HITCHHIKING
ADVENTURES

Two 16-year-olds thumbing the US coast-to-coast in 1970

R O B E R T   D R A K E

HITCHHIKING ADVENTURES
TWO 16-YEAR-OLDS THUMBING THE US COAST-TO-COAST IN 1970

iUniverse books may be ordered through booksellers or by contacting:

iUniverse
1663 Liberty Drive
Bloomington, IN 47403
www.iuniverse.com
844-349-9409

ISBN: 978-1-6632-5044-5 (sc)
ISBN: 978-1-6632-5042-1 (hc)
ISBN: 978-1-6632-5043-8 (e)

Library of Congress Control Number: 2023902639

Print information available on the last page.

iUniverse rev. date: 02/24/2023

For Mom and Dad.
This happened with your support in more ways than one.

INTRODUCTION

Over many years, at family gatherings and get-togethers with friends, I would occasionally tell a single story about an event that took place on this trip. I can't explain why, but I rarely shared these stories for the twenty-five years following the trip. But whenever I did share a hitchhiking episode, those who heard it wanted to hear more.

This journal is about a wild and incredible hitchhiking trip that took me from coast to coast and back again throughout the summer of 1970.

Before writing this journal, I had to decide how much I was willing to divulge. I decided to lay it out there naked (well, maybe with a fig leaf), telling it exactly as it happened, including—to borrow a movie title—the good, the bad, and the ugly. To the best of my memory, everything is revealed precisely as it happened, without exaggeration.

I recall these events because they were extraordinarily eye-opening for a sixteen-year-old, leaving quite an impression and ultimately becoming lifetime memories.

Yes, I realize that putting this story on paper could rule out any chance of my ever being elected president of the United States; the other disqualifiers are too numerous to list. Frankly, I'm not concerned.

Publishing this honest journal will likely come with consequences; it will reveal embarrassing events, moments of questionable judgment, and possibly the kinds of mistakes better left unknown and secret.

I am grateful to my parents, sons, brothers, and others who asked me to write the whole story about that summer's adventure. If they hadn't encouraged me, this entire event would have been forgotten, as though it had never happened, and I would not have had the thrill of reexperiencing that summer again.

More than fifty years later, here it is.

CHAPTER 1

THE GREAT HITCHHIKING TRIP

On a warm June night in 1970, four sixteen-year-old boys sat around a campfire, drinking somewhat cool beer. An underlying excitement was in the air since it was the last day of the school year. Finally, out for the summer!

A conversation began when I asked, "What are you guys doing this summer?"

Kevin replied, "I guess I could go with the family down to the shore for a week, but then I would spend most of the time minding my little sisters, and that's no fun."

Tommy said, "No plans at all," as he snapped open another beer.

Eddie said nothing about his summer intentions but suggested, "Let's go out to California."

The discussion evolved into an idea; it sounded like unrealistic talk, maybe even a fantasy. Wow, if we could make this dream real, it could be one incredible adventure!

The campfire was going dark, but we were lit.

The idea was to leave tomorrow morning to hitchhike from New Jersey (home) across the country to California and back again.

Why hitchhike? None of us had access to a car, much less a driver's license. Money, or lack thereof, was a problem. Hitchhiking was the only form of transportation that met our considerable restraints.

My name is Rob, and I was one of the four adventurous sixteen-year-old boys. This journal is an accurate log of what happened—what *really* happened.

Robert Drake

The Deal

We made the big decision between beers (which were becoming warm) that it was a go. We agreed we'd meet in front of Kevin's house at eight o'clock the next morning.

On my walk home from the campfire, I began getting nervous. I knew I had to ask for my parents' approval; I couldn't simply take off or leave a handwritten note.

I stewed about it. Suppose my parents said no? It would be not only a disappointment but also downright embarrassing. What would my friends think if I had to back out because my parents wouldn't let me go? Shit, that was a scary thought.

The house was quiet, which was not surprising, considering it was a little past midnight when I arrived home.

I have genuinely great parents, but I also knew this request would be a big ask. I was the oldest of four boys, so it wasn't as though my siblings had done anything like this before. It made me the Lewis and Clark of the offspring. So I sucked it in, took a deep breath, and went upstairs to my parents' bedroom door. I knew I would be waking them up, which was not going to make the conversation flow any easier.

I knocked on the door, and after a while, they woke and said, "Come in."

Feeling somewhat guilty for waking them, I decided to get straight to the point and explain how I wanted to spend the summer. I don't remember my exact words, but effectively, they were "I'm going to leave tomorrow morning and hitchhike out to California." I thought I might have more success by making it sound like a statement rather than a request for permission.

My statement-request took them from a comfortable sleep to a stunned, puzzled state of shock sprinkled with disbelief. They seemed unsure of what they were hearing.

"You want to what?"

I realized my initial request might have sounded as if I were going alone. I repeated my plan, this time sure to include the names of the other three kids so it would sound more like a group trip.

Then the questions came:

"Where are you going to sleep?"

"How and where are you going to eat?"

"How much money do you have?"

I responded to some of these questions with "Well, as for the sleep part, I guess we'll be camping at night, and I'll use the money I have to buy food."

My answers to the first two questions probably weren't the most convincing, but I was ready for the third. I would rely on the well-known Boy Scout motto, "Be prepared"—always be in a state of readiness in mind and body.

It was questionable that the "mind and body" part of the motto applied to me after an evening of smoking joints and drinking beer.

I said confidently, "I've got it covered. I have forty-six dollars." After I said it, I thought to myself, *Um, even I don't think it sounds like enough money to support myself through the summer.*

Soon it was negotiating time.

My mother was the first to question me. "What are you bringing? Do you need a suitcase? What clothes are you packing? What will you wear if it gets cold? What about pajamas? Should you bring a bathing suit?"

"Mom, stop. I know what to bring," I said firmly.

I had put a little thought into it, and I proceeded to outline that I would use my knapsack and bring my sleeping bag. "Mom, I can only fit so many items, and I will pack the important stuff that will fit. No to the bathing suit, and I haven't worn pajamas since I was six and don't plan to start now." I spoke with complete respect. This was no time to start even a slight disagreement.

Finally, both my parents were genuinely concerned about my safety.

"What would you do if you needed help for some reason, and how can we reach you to make sure you're OK?"

The deal agreed to was this: if I took the trip, I had to call home every Sunday to confirm I was alive and tell them my location. I frowned, unable to even imagine the cost of calling home (long distance) from phone booths each week.[1]

I would have to stretch my forty-six dollars over ten weeks. In 1970,

[1] Note to younger readers: In the 1970s, phone booths were public telephones that required the caller to pump in coins to keep the connection open. They were enormously popular and located everywhere.

there was no such thing as a cell phone. Long-distance calls were expensive, and the concept of unlimited calling did not yet exist, especially from a phone booth.

In short, we settled that I could call collect.[2]

A deal had been sealed! I was thrilled. It had been one exciting day and night. I went to my room and made a mental list that started with collecting my knapsack and sleeping bag and all the other articles I thought essential to bring.

I felt a hyperpsyched type of ready, with a sprinkle of the unknown.

Lying down to sleep, I looked at the alarm clock that I'd thought would be dead for the summer and realized I would need one more morning wake-up.

I was off to see America with no supervision.

---

[2] Irish eyes were smiling upon me.

CHAPTER 2

THE TIMES AND AN ERA

Before I reveal more about our hitchhiking venture, it might be helpful to briefly describe the environment and the culture—what life was like—when we embarked on our trip.

The 1960s were a time of much turmoil. Youth, especially the younger generation, rebelled to an extent never seen before. I remember my father—a member of the Greatest Generation—saying to friends, "It seems that every value we stand for is being challenged." And my parents' values indeed were.

The revolution was not subtle; it was evident globally in sweeping changes in the physical appearance of young adults and teens. Boys and men wore their hair long, often below the shoulders, and grew beards. Miniskirted women went braless and wore nose rings (as well as piercings in other parts of their anatomy!). And much to my delight, sexual restraints were loosened.

The 1969 moon landing was a moment of universal American pride that symbolized to every human on the planet what mankind was capable of, opening minds to future opportunities and recognition of achievement. As with other major life events, those who witnessed it will never forget where they were and what they were doing then. For me, it was a significant moment akin to the assassination of President Kennedy and 9/11.

Moon Landing, July 20, 1969 (courtesy of NASA).

A radical change took place in popular music. Ed Sullivan's enormously popular Sunday evening TV show introduced many upcoming future stars. Rock 'n' roll continued evolving, taking on huge names, such as the Beatles and numerous other bands, including duo and trio music groups who collectively reflected the times. The use of drugs, especially weed, became prevalent everywhere, particularly at concerts featuring contemporary bands. Woodstock is a classic example.

The causes of the cultural shift were many, but the war in Vietnam was a significant factor in dividing the nation. Only two months before our trip, the Ohio National Guard responded to quell protestors at Kent State University during a mass protest against the US bombing of Cambodia. Twenty-eight guardsmen fired more than sixty rounds for thirteen seconds, killing four students and wounding nine others. Some students killed were not protesting but simply walking on the campus.

Crosby, Stills, Nash, and Young's "Four Dead in Ohio" recorded the day in song, while an influential magazine portrayed photos of a shot student lying on the ground. In contrast, others depicted students seeking peace as they slid flowers into soldiers' gun barrels.

* * *

President Johnson successfully signed the Civil Rights Act of 1964, landmark civil rights and labor legislation outlawing discrimination based on race, color, religion, sex, and national origin. Over time, this considerably impacted advancing rights for African Americans and others.

America's civil rights evolved throughout the already tense 1960s. Civil rights protests, some violent, took place in all major American cities. The most respected protests were the peaceful ones led by Dr. Martin Luther

King Jr., an African American Baptist minister and activist. He became the most visible spokesperson and leader in the American civil rights movement. All had to respect his nonviolent approach.

At thirty-five, Martin Luther King Jr. was the youngest man to receive the Nobel Peace Prize.

His powerful nonviolent activism, ironically, resulted in his assassination in April 1968.

* * *

Also in 1968, presidential candidate Robert F. Kennedy, the younger brother of President John F. Kennedy, was shot while campaigning in Los Angeles. Earlier that evening, the forty-two-year-old junior senator from New York was declared the winner in the South Dakota and California Democratic Party primaries during the 1968 presidential election.

This was the rapidly changing climate in which the four of us set off. Some Americans accepted our culture, while others saw us as undisciplined hippies. We were long-haired, scruffy-looking kids with no idea what we were getting into.

The four boys in this story grew up during this turbulent decade.

DEPARTURE DAY

The four of us met the following morning as planned, and with excited anticipation, we set off to hit America's highways. Our adventure group consisted of the following:

Tommy Sidhad was a short guy with the longest hair of all of us. His mouth more than made up for his height since he never hesitated to speak his mind, regardless of whom he was talking to or what needed to be said. Tommy didn't hold back anything, and my guess is that he's still as vocal today as he was then.

Kevin Mellish was a lean skin-and-bones kind of kid with curly jet-black hair. His pleasant personality allowed him to make friends with everyone easily.

Ed "Fast Eddie" Quigs was the only one of the four of us I would describe as husky. He was the quietest of the group and the person you would least want to get in a fight with.

I, Rob (Bob) Drake, had recently moved to the area in the middle of my sophomore school year, making me the new kid. I had met Tommy a few months prior in several classes we attended, while I first had met Fast Eddie and Kevin at the campfire last night.

The shared sense of excitement had built inside each of us. An obvious symptom: we couldn't stop talking while covering a range of subjects, primarily the unlimited possibilities in front of us.

Before last night, this trip was something none of us had ever considered doing.

It was a banner day, with a blue sky, sunshine, and ultracomfortable mid-June temperatures. It was a picture-perfect day.

* * *

While on his way to work, my father dropped us off on the Interstate Route 80 West entrance ramp.

Each of us had a large knapsack filled with what we thought at the time were essential supplies, plus a sleeping bag. We had accurately anticipated the need to rough it sometimes. I gained immediate popularity by being the only one who'd thought to bring a roll of toilet paper.

Our eagerness to get started was at an all-time high. That excitement was most evident when we all seemed to be talking about our upcoming adventure simultaneously. Some enthusiasm probably came from embarking on this kind of journey without any clear-cut destination or route. Regardless, we were launching off to see America!

That first day was slow going; we began realizing that getting rides would be much more challenging than we'd anticipated.

We quickly determined that the driver made the call to stop—or not. Passengers had little or nothing to do with the decision.

I also learned that it helped to look the driver of the approaching car directly in the eye, hoping that some type of contact could be made. If a driver looked back to check us out, it was usually a good indication that he might be considering stopping for us.

We quickly realized that cars had space limits, making it understandable why some drivers simply couldn't add another four passengers (with backpacks) even if they wanted to. For some drivers, the thought of picking up four sixteen-year-old boys, strangers, was too much to consider, such as the school bus that passed by us loaded with children. Possibly we were more than most drivers wanted to take a chance on, especially as a group of long-haired teenagers. We obviously weren't choirboys on our way to a church picnic.

While we waited for a long time in the same place for a ride, I asked, "How did it go with your parents? You know, them letting you go on this trip?"

Kevin said, "My parents are getting divorced and couldn't care less. I didn't tell them I was going, since they won't care."

Fast Eddie said, "I told my mom"—Fast Eddie didn't have a dad—"that I got invited to summer camp by a friend from school, and then their family asked me to join them on their two-week vacation. I figured that would cover me for a month."

Tommy didn't want to talk about it.

CHAPTER 4

CALLING IT A DAY

The last ride of our first day dropped us off at the I-80 exit for Lock Haven, Pennsylvania. It was well after eight o'clock, and the sun was starting to set. While we had covered a decent amount of ground, we decided to call it a day. We were hungry and feeling tired from the previous late night, so we started walking toward the town center.

We began asking people near our age if they knew of a location where we could stay for the night around town.

The first person we asked was probably a college girl, who responded with a dirty look, as if we were a gang of known serial rapists. She only acknowledged us by flashing us a quick, terrified face, followed by moving in the opposite direction as fast as possible.

After getting rejected by the following two people, we asked a guy who paused, thought for a few seconds, and then said, "Follow me, and let's check on something." We followed him onto a nice, quiet residential street and entered the front door of a large, older house. Some young men were hanging around in a large room, talking and laughing—a real party atmosphere. Shortly after, we learned that it was a college fraternity house. I thought, *Cool! I have never been in one of these before.*

We continued to follow our new friend, who took us to meet a huge, muscle-bound, tall man he introduced as John. Our new friend pointed to the four of us and told John we were looking for a place to sleep for the night. As we looked up at John, I realized none of us had yet uttered a word. John welcomed us with a friendly smile and instructed our new friend to set us up in a particular room upstairs. As we headed upstairs,

John said, "Oh, before you go, we're having a party here tonight. You're welcome to join us."

I looked back at him and said, "Sounds good; we'll be there." Our first night out was starting to look good.

We walked into our sizeable, clean room with two bunk beds already made. Perfect—we each had our own bed!

Over the last two minutes, the encounter had given us a renewed sense of adventure, similar to the way we'd felt when we started that morning. It was our first night out. Now we had our room with beds and a party lined up at a college fraternity house.

We didn't know it at the time, but the next time we would sleep in an actual bed would be in Cheyenne, Wyoming.

Things were looking up.

* * *

Many students attended Lock Haven University to be part of the Lock Haven Bald Eagles' highly regarded championship wrestling team. The Bald Eagles' wrestling program participated in the NCAA Division I, and in 1970, John was president of the college's largest fraternity consisting of all wrestlers.

After getting set up in our new digs, we returned downstairs to check out the party. It was somewhat different from high school parties (at least during our time). The usual music was playing, but the extra feature was the large keg of beer sitting on ice in the middle of the room. On the wall was a large emblem labeled *Bald Eagles*. Everyone was drinking, and some frat guys were in the company of some delightful girls. John spotted us and asked if we wanted a beer. He didn't have to ask twice. He pointed to the large plastic cups and said, "Help yourself."

This guy John was shooting up the charts as far as we were concerned. He had set us up with a nice place to sleep for the night and fed us some refreshing, cold beer.

Will every night be like this?

We were seriously thirsty, so the cold beer hit the spot. We hadn't eaten anything since breakfast at home before we left. The one beer quickly went straight to our heads and had us feeling good.

* * *

It was probably close to nine in the evening when we all felt it was time to get some food.

Previously, we passed a diner when following our new friend on the way to the fraternity house. It was no more than a hundred yards away from the frat house, so we left the party to address the hunger issue.

The waitress was friendly, considering that we tried to limit our order to a single dollar. She briefly rolled her eyes while taking our order, probably imagining how she would spend all the windfall tip money.

Our drink order consisted of water since it was free, appropriately fitting our budget, and we knew beer awaited us back at the party.[3] The food was good because it put a dent in the hungry feeling you get when your stomach starts screaming, "Hey, give me some damn food—like now!"

It had been an exciting day, we finally were getting something to eat, and the beer party was topping things off.

Was today too good to be true?

Mostly younger people filled the diner, a hangout for a summer evening crowd, including some profoundly attractive girls who didn't appear to be future nuns. The diner's jukebox was pumping out hit pop songs from the '60s, so we had to raise our voices for our conversations to be heard. Suddenly, Kevin got up and left the booth without saying a word. The three of us looked over to see where he was going. Ah, it quickly became apparent. Kevin suddenly stopped at another booth after taking about fifteen steps. We all could see why.

The four good-looking girls in the other booth said it all. They were probably college coeds. Beer notwithstanding, we had to give Kevin credit for having the guts to approach the girls.

Our attention was riveted on Kevin and the girl he seemed focused on. While we couldn't hear what they were saying, Kevin appeared to be successful at trying to be charming. He was smiling and looked like he was having a good time. The girls looked as if Kevin had entranced them, giggling at everything he said. I don't know about the other guys, but I wished I could hear what he said—maybe I could have picked up some tips. Kevin appeared to be putting on an outstanding performance. He was probably closer to experiencing intimacy tonight than all of us combined.

---

[3] Four sixteen-year-old boys (consuming alcohol underage) roaming the USA—what could possibly go wrong?

That was when the shit hit the fan.

As we watched Kevin and the girls, four or five guys entered the diner and appeared to be looking around, perhaps for a table or booth. After not paying attention at first, many people turned around to see a good-looking, nicely-dressed guy with brown hair. He was about five foot ten, wearing a brown fishnet-type shirt. Everyone looked at him because he started screaming at the top of his lungs—at Kevin! Everyone in the diner turned to see what all the commotion was about.

Kevin looked at Fishnet Guy, baffled.

It was clear this guy was furious—in fact, so livid his face started to change to a darker color.

I'll leave out some of the fouler language, but he ripped into Kevin for being a subhuman life-form (or something close to it) that could only compare with some type of animal excrement.

Shit, this is getting out of hand.

I had no idea how other people in the diner felt, but we were in awe; we had no idea why this stranger, seemly recognized by all in the restaurant, appeared ready to kill our debonair friend.

Hell, how much trouble could we have gotten into? We had only been in town for about an hour. I didn't realize at the time that the situation hadn't even started. All the commotion was beginning to cause some alarming concern.

What the hell is going on?

Then Fishnet Guy got in Kevin's face. The incident started to look ugly. Kevin looked at Fishnet and was speechless.

Then everything became clear with one statement: Fishnet accused Kevin of having a romantic interlude with his girlfriend. He then advised Kevin that he would personally sever his dick.

Kevin's romantic moves had lit a powder keg. The entire diner picked up on the brewing dispute as Fishnet's volume increased. The possibility of a nasty confrontation gripped all the diner's patrons. The potential fight changed the diner from a noisy place to a library. There was total silence, except for Fishnet and the jukebox music.

The waitresses and busboys congregated at the counter, intently watching.

While Fishnet was in Kevin's face, he strongly suggested they "take this outside." They did, so we bolted out after our friend to help him—in case he wanted an assist. Unfortunately, so did Fishnet's friends. Watching things unfold, we saw that not only was Kevin outnumbered, but so were all four of us!

The four New Jersey boys confronted Fishnet and his gang of hoodlums. It then turned into an all-out fight. The guy who approached me was ready for a good Saturday night fight. I thought a peaceful resolution had to be possible, so I said, "Hey, look, I'm sure we can settle this without fighting."

Not having been in this situation before, without waiting to comment on my request, the hoodlum immediately threw a right fist into my face, temporarily knocking me out. Real or imagined, I vaguely thought I heard him laugh as I collapsed on the street.

Seconds later, I woke to find myself lying in the middle of the quiet street, and although hazy, I started to assess the situation. Kevin and Eddie were holding their own. Tommy was lying on his back, taking a beating. I saw that his arm was extended back and away from him, and he held in his right hand an open pocketknife! It was dark enough that the attackers didn't notice it. He could have done severe damage with one swipe, but he made no attempt to use it.

I have to get help.

My senses were coming back, and the adrenaline was now pumping. I ran as fast as possible the short distance to the frat house, swung open the front door, and screamed as loudly as I could, "John! John, they are killing my friends! They're killing my friends!"

Now I had the cavalry behind me! About twenty big college guys followed me, running full speed to the scene. They picked up on what was happening instantly.

Fishnet and his friends quickly realized that now *they* were seriously outnumbered; plus, these were not people to mess with. That cognitive calculation was too late for Fishnet—all his buddies seemed to have vanished.

All activity came to a dead halt.

Fortunately for us, the tables had turned.

John and his friends must have been familiar with these guys from prior incidents.

Bright lights outside of the diner lit up the parking lot. That was where the incident concluded. There must have been more than thirty people in the parking lot, all waiting to see what would happen. Everyone who'd been in the diner was now in the parking lot. They got a show.

John didn't waste any time getting to Fishnet. Now it was John who was pissed off. John grabbed Fishnet's shirt with both hands and lifted him so high that his feet were dangling at least three feet off the ground. Fishnet's face showed fear, possibly to the point that he might lose control of bodily functions right then and there. I will never forget the words John said while holding him up so that they were eye to eye: "Don't you ever lay a fucking hand on my friends again. Is that clear?"[4]

Fishnet nodded speechlessly, as if to say, *Yeah, whatever you want.*

With the damage John's clenched fists did to Fishnet's shirt, one could safely conclude that he would never wear it again, except for an indoor painting job.

Then two police cars simultaneously roared into the parking lot with lights flashing as John let Fishnet drop down to the ground. When the police arrived, the crowd quickly broke up. The college wrestling team and the four Jersey boys walked back to the now hypercharged party for some more cold beer. Our partying lasted until the adrenaline wore off, and we couldn't keep our eyes open.

As I put my head on the pillow, I summarized the first day's events, thinking about the fight with Fishnet and his band of hometown punks.

I trailed off while fantasizing about the future, imagining that Fishnet and his girlfriend patched things up and got married a month after the birth of their first of five children.

For the next twenty or so years, they lived in a rusted-out rented trailer nicely equipped with plumbing and electricity, just a few miles from the diner.

Despite infrequent trips to the diner (food stamps sponsored by the US Department of Agriculture weren't accepted there), over time, the couple's clothing sizes expanded to XXL dimensions to accommodate the girth, all of which was added after that night's incident.

Fishnet moved from job to job, limited by any desire for advancement or financial assurance. He felt comfort and security in the feeling that the government would provide his family with food, medical care, and subsidized trailer rental support. Since the government medical care did not include dental coverage, the couple's missing teeth told much of their story.

Fishnet generally thought that all was fine; life had just dealt him a dirty diaper, and eventually, one of those lottery tickets had to hit, someday.

---

[4] Wow, we were friends, or was he just making a point?

PAIRS

We woke up after sleeping later than expected the following day, but hey, we didn't have school, so no worries. My face felt a little better from the effect of the punch I had taken last night. At least I had all my teeth, although I kept checking with my tongue to make sure.

After packing up our knapsacks and rolling up our sleeping bags, we were ready to start day two. As we left the fraternity house, we all decided we owed the guys a big thank-you. We went looking for John but learned he wasn't there, so we made sure to thank other frat brothers and begged them to share with John our appreciation for his letting us have a place to sleep, inviting us to their party, and, most of all, saving our asses last night from the local townies.

* * *

It was a sterling, sunny day as we started our one-mile trek back to the highway ramp, sticking our thumbs out for each passing car as we walked. Kevin's frustration showed as he screamed at a passing car, "What is your damn problem?" Without making a sound, the driver responded to Kevin's question by sticking his arm out the car window with one of his fingers extended.

We got excited when one car did stop, only to get let down when we realized that we and our gear would never fit, forcing us to pass on the ride. How exasperating.

Our conversation revolved around how difficult getting rides was, and we had only been at it for twenty-four hours. It not only was aggravating but also had become a problem.

Eddie said, "Why don't we break up into pairs? It should be much easier to get rides that way."

We tossed around Eddie's idea, and while no one liked the idea of splitting up, we all concluded that if we did, we'd get farther faster.

Together we planned to meet up at a predetermined location each night. We decided to split up, continuing our trip in pairs.

Arriving at the Lock Haven Interstate 80 West ramp, the four of us gathered around Kevin, who had our sole paper map. With it spread out on the ramp asphalt, we got down on our hands and knees, each trying to get a good look at it. We decided we'd meet that night at the exit ramp for Milan, Ohio.[5] Tommy and I made one pair, while Kevin and Eddie became the other duo.

That was the last time Tommy and I saw Kevin, Eddie, or the map for the remainder of the trip.

Things moved lickety-split with only the two of us thumbing rides. Rides now came more frequently, allowing us to cover more ground in less time. One ride took us west across the rest of Pennsylvania and into Ohio, over the Ohio River. We had recently heard about the Ohio River catching fire![6]

Since our planned destination was California, the rapid succession of rides was encouraging. As passengers, we were often asked, "Where are you kids going?"

---

[5] Paper maps were used before the Global Positioning System (GPS). The US Department of Defense launched satellites to make GPS fully operational for use by the military. In the 1980s, GPS was functioning for commercial use, and it became useable for everyone in 1993.

Prior to GPS, everyone used paper maps. These maps outlined where roads went and required one to analyze and make decisions on where to travel. A paper map was what one used to navigate, an absolute requirement for each auto. Maps have been in use since the sixth century BC.

[6] According to *Smithsonian* magazine, Cleveland emerged as a significant manufacturing center, and the river became heavily affected by industrial pollution, so much so that it caught fire at least thirteen times, most famously on June 22, 1969, which helped spur the American environmental movement.

Our answer was proud: "California." It was an impressive answer that usually made me smile.

A driver who picked us up in Ohio said, "I can get you to Indiana."

He drove at alarming speeds. Quietly, I told Tommy, "This guy is in a real hurry."

He said, "Yeah, he's probably got a hot date."

Obviously, Tommy knew what a "hot date" was, but at the time, perhaps somewhat naive, I didn't fully understand what that meant.

I thought this was great. *We're cooking with oil now! Another new state.*

I'm sure Tommy and I were thinking about the same thing—meeting up with Kevin and Fast Eddie. We whispered to each other, not wanting the driver to hear our dilemma, and realized we weren't sure which exit number in Ohio we'd agreed to meet at.

"Do you remember the exit number?" I asked.

"No, I just remember the exit name began with an *M*," Tommy said.

Somewhat discouraged and feeling a tinge of guilt for not holding up our end of the plan, we decided to sit tight, make the most of our current ride, and continue onward. We hoped it was the right decision.

We were beginning to realize our plan to meet up each afternoon or evening was unrealistic.

It was dark when the ride dropped us off in northeast Indiana at a major interchange, with the Michigan border a few miles north of us. It had taken six hours to get from our last ride in Ohio to Indiana, including a few stops for the bathroom, fuel refill, and a truck stop diner for food.[7] We had covered significant mileage that day.

Once we were out of the car and free to talk, I shared with Tommy how disappointed I was that our plan to meet up with Kevin and Eddie had failed. Tommy understood how I felt but shrugged, saying, "Well, there is nothing we can do about it now, so let's just move on."

---

[7] I'm proud to say we did a good job in adhering to the dollar-a-day budgeted food allowance. It helped that Tommy and I viewed our financial approach the same. Conceitedly, I had one or two dollars left when I arrived home.

CHAPTER 6

INDIANA WAS MEAN

We found ourselves at an interchange where two main interstate highways intersected: I-80 went east and west from New York City to San Francisco, and I-69 ran north and south from Indianapolis to Flint, Michigan. It had numerous entrance and exit ramps.

Bright lights mounted on top of towering poles lit the entire interchange area.

Our goal was to get back on Route 80 West the following day. Since it was around ten o'clock at night, we planned to look for a place to roll out our sleeping bags nearby.

We suddenly noticed signs warning that convicted hitchhikers would be skinned alive, roasted like dead rats, fined, and whipped; plus, if the judge didn't like them, face serious prison time. Since there was no mention of waterboarding, we weren't too worried.

We spotted a toll booth with a group of young people standing near it. We decided to check it out.

As cars approached the toll booths, we saw a broad paved area thirty by fifty feet on the right side in front of the small brick booth office. Upon our arrival, we met fellow hitchhikers there. They referred to that wide section of pavement with an extended shoulder, safely out of the way of traffic, as the "waiting area." The group assembled there since it was safe and free of traffic, as all vehicles queued up in separate lanes upon approaching the toll booths. At the time, toll booths handled cash for all vehicles, while years later, cost-saving technology, such as E-ZPass, sped the toll booth process along and saved manpower.

The area worked well, as cars slowed down anyway as they approached the toll booths.

Each person or group arriving was assigned a number. We were twenty-three and twenty-four, and we soon learned that number seven was up to catch the next ride. As we waited our turn, we were impressed at how orderly the process was. It was an exemplary system that worked well.

The process was going to take a while. Since no cars traveled in the waiting area, it was a safe place to hang out while waiting for your number to come up. When it did, it was your turn to stick out your thumb. We all felt a touch of encouragement when a car stopped to pick up hitchhikers.

Around midnight, I had a conversation with a fellow a couple of years older than I was. Like us, he was waiting his turn to hitch a ride. His destination was Canada. The draft board had notified him that he had to report for duty in the armed forces. He said, "Reporting for duty means I'll be shipped off to Vietnam after I learn how to use an M16," an automatic weapon. He would leave the USA for Canada, choosing not to serve, which made him a draft dodger.[8]

The traffic gradually curtailed as the evening grew into the night. Sometime between eleven at night and one in the morning, traffic dwindled to almost nothing. The toll takers were reduced from ten when we initially arrived, down to two. Ah, the night shift had showed up.

The collective group of hitchhikers decided to call it a day and get some sleep, less the few who had numbers close to coming up soon.

We all rolled out our sleeping bags in our unique, paved safe-zone area. As I fell asleep, I wondered, *Why are the damn crickets so loud? Will I ever be able to sleep?* That thought was the last thing I remembered.

Sleeping soundly, I was oblivious when, sometime around three in the morning, an Indiana State Police car pulled up alongside the sleeping group. I continued my stone-cold sleep as everyone followed the officer's demand to "Wake up, and get your fucking stuff off the road—now!"

All complied except for one person—me. I continued to sleep through it all in my sleeping bag.

Tommy later told me that despite his assuring the officer he would wake me up, the cop snickered at him and said, "Back off, kid. I'll take care of this." The cop had everyone's attention. The interaction between Tommy

---

[8] A draft dodger is a person who illegally avoids joining the armed forces.

and the cop intensified, holding the attention of the entire group of twenty-plus people. Now all awake, they watched to see how the incident would go down. The cop drove the police car close to and alongside my sleeping bag. With only inches between the police car and me, the cop blasted the siren!

Some people watching later told me they were amazed; when the cop hit the siren, the entire sleeping bag, with me in it, horizontally levitated six inches off the ground and then fell back flat on the pavement. To this day, I am not sure if it was the siren or falling on the hard pavement that woke me. Probably a combination of both.

I sat bolt upright and looked out from the top of my sleeping bag in my hazed state. In front of my face, a gold emblem, a shield, on the side door of a police car read, "Indiana State Police."

Where the hell did this come from?

A cop wearing a round Mountie-type hat was babbling something at me, but I didn't comprehend a single word he said. I am sure I appeared in a state of shock, half asleep, or both.

Fifty years later, the word *Indiana* still gives me a mild taste of nausea.[9]

Later in the morning the following day, our numbers finally came up. It was now our turn to get a ride out of there. As far as I was concerned, we couldn't get out of Indiana fast enough. We continued our journey on I-80 West. Signs kept pointing out that we would eventually arrive in Chicago.

We were unaware that we crossed from the eastern into the central time zone halfway through Indiana.

---

[9] Throughout the trip, drivers often had their car radios on. One of the big hit pop songs that continuously played over and over again was "Indiana Wants Me." For fifty years, I have been humming along the wrong words: "Indiana was mean." My lyrical interpretation might have been wrong, but my feelings about the state were dead-on.

CHAPTER 7

THE ILLINOIS RUSTBELT

As we crossed the line into Illinois, we left one ride and quickly got another. The plump man driving was primarily bald and needed a shave (no need to tell us he wasn't on a diet). The talkative guy told us he was going to Schaumburg. Realizing we weren't familiar with that region of the country, he explained that Schaumburg was a suburb of Chicago.

He was incredibly proud of his role as an architect of what would become Illinois's largest mall, which would significantly impact the area; conceivably, it could contain up to one hundred stores. He felt that the opening of the new mall would have an impact similar to NASA's first manned space launch. While we did think one hundred was a significant number of stores, we didn't share the same enthusiasm as the plump man and started to look forward to getting out when he took his exit.

We told him we were going to California by taking Interstate 80 westbound. He said if we wanted, he could take us up to Interstate 90, which also headed west and was his route to Schaumburg. Hey, we were flexible, and a ride was a ride. It wasn't as if we had any particular place to be, so we said, "Sure, man."

God only knew where Kevin and Eddie were. I tried to figure out a way we could reconnect, but I concluded that it was unlikely we would ever see them again, at least that summer.

With the Interstate 90 decision made, we took an exit leaving 80 and got on a new highway heading north on a loop around the outside of the city of Chicago. Mr. Plump turned out to be a nice guy and took several exits out of his planned destination to get us up to 90 West. At the exit for

Skokie, he pulled over and let us out at the entrance ramp for Interstate 90. He wished us luck and safety on our excursion of the USA, and we could easily detect the genuine sincerity in his words.

Our next ride was from a businessman wearing a dress shirt and tie. His suit jacket hung from the hook above the rear door, blocking my window view since I was sitting in the backseat. I quietly moved his sturdy tan leather-bound briefcase toward the door, allowing more room for my legs. He proudly announced that he was going to Rockford, as if it were a major US city akin to Washington, DC. Tommy and I looked at each other, wondering what and where Rockford was. We didn't know that Rockford was the largest city in Illinois besides the Chicago metropolitan area.[10]

The ride continued to take us west on Interstate 90, so all was well.

Mr. Businessman dropped us off at the exit for Rockford, which was in north-central Illinois.

On our next ride, Tommy said, "Bob, did you see that sign we just passed? It says we are on 90 North!"

As I calculated Tommy's observation, red lights started flashing. Alarmed, I thought, *Wait a second. We wanted to be—were supposed to be—going west. What's happening?*

Shortly after, we got a ride in a pickup truck from a man who assured us that 90 bent toward the west a few hundred miles ahead. Similar to the start of most rides, we asked the driver where he was going. He told us he was headed to a farm slightly north of Madison.

Madison turned out to be a city in Wisconsin—the Cheese State.

We started seeing signs for Wisconsin. Maybe Madison was there. Then the question was, where exactly was Wisconsin? I knew Wisconsin was a state, but I was not exactly sure where.

In grammar school, I had taken several geography classes. I always had done well in them, probably getting some of my best grades in those courses. I believed I had more than an adequate working knowledge of the places and locations around me, not only good marks.

I could point out Europe on a globe, as well as South America, Africa, the USSR, and even the small continents of Australia and Antarctica.

---

[10] Rockford is a community that is about as safe as the South Bronx in New York City at night and likely, according to FBI violent crime statistics, maintains a similar murder rate.

Why didn't I have a clue where states and cities right here in America were located? I felt a genuine disappointment in my grammar school education teachers. I concluded that my lack of education had nothing to do with my missed classes, missed homework, lack of interest, or poor test results. Since I had always been a model student deserving to be placed on a pedestal (a legend in my own mind), I felt I had the right to blame my educators for anything making me appear less than perfect.[11]

The conversation was always the same when we caught a new ride, such as our interest in the driver's destination (how far the ride would take us). The driver usually asked questions, such as our names, where we were from, how long we had been traveling, and whether we were packing heat. Just kidding—they didn't ask that last one. Many of the questions were to feel out the young men they were giving a ride to, and in some cases, they hoped we could carry on a conversation to help keep them awake. When we told them we were from New Jersey, the response typically was amazement and disbelief that these two kids were so far from home.

As we spent time riding in the pickup truck, not something I had often done, we learned more—this man liked to talk. He could go on and on nonstop about a whole range of topics.

We crossed the state line from Illinois to Wisconsin.

That particular pickup truck driver did not need us to keep him awake. All he needed was someone capable of listening and still breathing.[12] Some of what he had to say might have put another farmer to sleep; however, for us it was entertaining. He mainly spoke about farm life, the process and timing seeds are planted, types of fertilizers, how livestock and poultry are fed and tended, regular milking of cows, and assistance in breeding farm animals, including artificial insemination of livestock. He continued telling fascinating stories of farm animal and human interactions, all astonishing and different from the suburban New York City area.

Since we had gotten in the pickup, the signs had indicated we were going north, which never seemed to change, giving us mild concern. We hoped *West* would start showing up on signs soon.

---

[11] I have found in life that people who blame everyone other than themselves are usually the ones most responsible for their own problems.

[12] Maybe he frequently talked to himself so much that his friends and family started questioning his mental well-being.

As we approached Madison, the city's lights made the sky's stars fade into darkness. As we rode past the east side of Madison, there were many closely spaced exit and entrance ramps. Tommy and I knew this wouldn't be an area to camp in. Since he was close to his destination, we politely asked the pickup man to drop us off a short distance from the city where we could camp. He indicated a section of wooded land near the farm, away from buildings and roads. Although he wasn't sure, he said he thought it might be a reasonable area to camp and would be happy to let us off there. He had our gratitude, and we said a sincere "Thank you." We always let those who gave us rides know how much we genuinely appreciated the lift.

We were in complete darkness when we climbed out of the pickup truck with our knapsacks and sleeping bags. There was no roadway lighting. Our problem was seeing, since we didn't have a flashlight.

We walked off the road, and gradually, our eyes adjusted to the darkness. We were surrounded primarily by tall grass, so we walked about thirty to forty feet away from the quiet night highway and rolled out our sleeping bags to go to sleep. Looking up at the sky, I was amazed at how many stars were visible and how bright they were!

Within the next sixty seconds, Tommy and I were both sound asleep.

The sunrise woke us up early the next morning. Highway traffic noise had noticeably increased as the world started its new day. We rolled up our sleeping bags, and while we hiked our way back to the highway, Tommy said, "My stomach is hurting, and I'm not sure how far I can walk."

He was clearly hurting, and I thought he might need a doctor. *How could we get help if he needs it?*

"I'm hungry. Do you think getting something to eat would help?" I asked. We agreed that hunger could be the problem and that we needed to get something to eat soon.

We decided to get off at the first exit, regardless of how far the ride was going. We had to get something to eat. A caveat was that it had to be either a Burger King or a McDonald's. We'd consider something else if it was equally as cheap.

Tommy and I were both in the same financial shape. Our combined food allowance was a dollar a day.

I will never know how far we could have gone if we had chosen to stay with that first ride of the day, but we were going to stop for food regardless.

We'd not eaten anything since the day before, so the situation was serious. How serious? At that point, I would have—and this is hard to say—eaten fruitcake with a side of Spam.

We saw a sign on the fourth exit that indicated a fast-food restaurant, so we got off there. As always, we profusely thanked the driver for the ride, and then we hiked into town. We arrived at more of a hamlet than a town, which worked fine since it had a small diner. The trip taught me that water was free and to fill up on it when we could and use our one dollar on anything that would come close to filling our stomachs (vitamins, minerals, and an overall healthy diet were irrelevant).

During that summer, Tommy and I viewed eating from six perspectives.

1. Our scholarly background in finance and economics taught us that budgeting a dollar a day for food was essential for survival. Meals consisting of steak and lobster would not fit into our budget.
2. Our budget ruled out all dining establishments that took reservations.
3. We needed to use our budgeted amount for nourishment, although there were several times when we deviated from our planned budget.
4. The only places where we were likely to eat were inexpensive fast food places, typically hamburger chains, such as Burger King and McDonald's. At least one of these places seemed conveniently located at every other exit along America's highways. These establishments offered two burgers for less than a dollar and still left room for a single order of fries. We ate that same meal almost every day.[13]
5. The trip taught me that water was free and to fill up on it when I could.
6. I learned there was a (sometimes subtle) difference between feeling full and eating enough for life sustenance. Both were more important than eating food that tasted good—well, maybe close to good.

We felt better after eating and headed back out to the highway. Our next ride, another pickup truck, happened remarkably quickly. Tommy

---

[13] I doubt this diet included the minimum daily requirements of vitamins and minerals recommended by the FDA, but we managed to live.

and I squeezed into the cab seat with our knapsacks on our knees. I could picture the farmhand's work lifting, hoisting, and stacking heavy bales of hay onto the pickup truck bed.

The young driver couldn't have been any older than we were. After we went through the initial introductions and assessed where each was going, we asked him how old he was. He smiled and said, "Sixteen." He told us he'd gotten his driving permit at fourteen after taking a driver's ed course. He'd needed that permit then to get around and transport things on the farm. Sixteen was the age when a person could get a standard driver's license in Wisconsin. "Between us, I really was driving on the farm for years before getting my permit. All you've got to do is be breathing—well, and have your feet reach the pedals—to drive on the farm," he said.

He told us his family owned a dairy farm with a considerable quantity of cows. He chuckled at my question "How do you get the milk from the cows?" He explained machines called milkers were designed to extract the milk from the dairy cows. He told us about the pasteurization and homogenization of raw milk and other products, such as cheese, which also came from cow's milk.

It wasn't long before we realized Interstate 90, instead of going north, was starting to bend westward. I heaved a sigh of relief, thinking, *Good. At last, we are back on track again.*

We started to see signs for La Crosse, Wisconsin, and Minnesota. Our high school had a lacrosse team, although I had no idea how the game was played or even what the objective was.

On we went for hours, passing countless dairy farms.

* * *

Anyone with a remote interest in football will be familiar with the Green Bay Packers, whose home is in Green Bay, Wisconsin. "The Green Bay Packers were founded in 1919 by former high-school football rivals Earl 'Curly' Lambeau and George Whitney Calhoun. Lambeau solicited funds for uniforms from his employer, the Indian Packing Company. The Green

Bay Packers have played longer than any other NFL team in their original city."[14]

The first Super Bowl was played in 1967, with Green Bay winning the first and second Super Bowl games. Their legendary coach, Vince Lombardi, would become an icon of Super Bowl history. Each team who won the monumental game after that won the Lombardi Trophy.

Since my mother told me the football legend I saw on TV, Vince Lombardi, was her eighth-grade math teacher at Saint Cecilia's school in Englewood, New Jersey, I felt a connection to the man, albeit a long-distance one. Lombardi taught math classes and also was the coach of the high school football team.

All of that had me looking for the exit sign that said, "Green Bay."

Green Bay was in northeast Wisconsin, hundreds of miles from where we were. Consequently, I never saw a Green Bay sign. Based on NFL football games I'd seen, I suspected it could have been snowing and -8 degrees there, despite being late June.

---

[14] *Wikipedia*, last edited on 26 December 2022
http:// https://en.wikipedia.org/wiki/Green_Bay_Packers

CHAPTER 8

LAND OF TEN THOUSAND LAKES

Immediately after passing La Crosse, Wisconsin, we went over a bridge with a sign that said, "Mississippi River." That was a landmark. I had heard about this river forever but now saw it for the first time.

My eyes carefully focused on watching the river. I was expecting something extraordinary, but it was just a river, not even a big one at that. I was disappointed, thinking, *What's the big deal?* Halfway across the bridge, another sign read, "Entering Minnesota." Shortly after we crossed the bridge, a second sign said, "Welcome to Minnesota: Land of 10,000 Lakes." Another state—all of this felt good. We were making progress and continuing our westward travel.

Shortly after, he advised us we would soon reach the end of the road with him. We came across a sign for a state forest. It was getting late in the day, and we needed a break from the bumpy pickup truck. The state forest sounded like a good place to roll out our sleeping bags for the night. Soon an exit came up with an arrow sign indicating that this was the one to take for the forest. Once again, Tommy and I clambered out of the pickup truck with all our gear, ensuring our new young friend knew how grateful we were for the ride. As we got out of the truck, we saw a forest of tall trees, which we figured had to be the forest. We hiked down the exit ramp directly toward the trees.

As we got into our sleeping bags, we talked about how hungry we were—again. This time, we felt a little better, realizing what we felt was not a medical problem but, rather, the feeling of hunger pains; that we knew how to take care of. Food would have to wait till the morning.

The following day, sunlight visibly streamed through the trees, filtered by the roof of leaves. Since neither of us had a watch, we often had no idea what time it was, but it felt early, like most summer mornings.

I'd probably slept extraordinarily well due to the thick bed of leaves beneath our sleeping bags. While rolling up my bag, I was amazed at how many leaves ended up inside my bag. I made a mental note that I would have to clean it before using the sleeping bag the next night. My motto at that point in time was "If you don't have to do it today, put it off until tomorrow."

As soon as we got to the highway, we stuck our thumbs out, and almost immediately, a car pulled over to give us a ride. It was a two-door sedan, so getting the backseat rider and our gear into the back was a cumbersome process to pull off. Seeing the hassle we were having, the driver shut off the engine, got out of the car, opened the trunk, and helped load all our gear into the car trunk.

Placing our luggage in the trunk happened several times, and each time made me a little nervous; when the ride ended, the driver, intentionally or simply forgetting, could have taken off before we got our stuff out of the trunk. Fortunately for us, that scenario never happened.

After climbing into the huge car, we felt comfortable without having to manage the gear. The driver sported a long beard and plenty of tattoos. He told us he was only going to the next exit. We asked if there was a restaurant there. He said, "Yeah, I think there is a McDonald's there."

After the five-mile ride, Beard Man dropped us off at an exit that didn't have a McDonald's but did have a no-name fast food joint.

We were prepared to order our standard under-a-dollar burger package but instead heard, "Sorry, but we are only serving our breakfast menu now."

Major disappointment.

Hunger won: for a sum of ninety cents, we ordered two "quick breakfast" sandwiches, which tasted like shit. The meals included a coffee each. We got all of that under our essential budgeted dollar-a-day food allotment.[15]

Since we'd left Pennsylvania, obtaining good rides seemed to be going smoothly. That morning, things changed to slow motion; each lift went only one or two exits for the entire morning.

---

[15] I'm sure dog food would have tasted better and possibly been more nourishing.

We continued west on Interstate 90 across the entire state of Minnesota.

At that point, I realized if we went straight west, I had no idea which state we would enter next.

Interstate 90 ran directly east and west along the southern border of Minnesota. South of the Minnesota line was Iowa. I knew that because numerous signs alerted drivers to the exit for Somewhere, Iowa.

I was excited just to see geography: the scenery, ground formations, and various terrains, such as mountains and deserts. While I had not yet seen many of those environment types, the vast flat farmlands of the Midwest made a significant impact. The sight was beyond anything I had ever seen before, especially the farms' organized rows of green plants running from state to state for hundreds of miles. They reminded me of the systematized arrangement of gravestones in Arlington National Cemetery.[16]

I noticed that people dressed differently there; for example, overalls seemed the standard farmer attire. I saw numerous farm vehicles, such as tractors. Much of my fascination came from recognizing the differences between the midwestern states and New Jersey. Please pardon the repetition, but this observation continued to happen repeatedly. It was boring to see so many farms for so long. Still, seeing that land and knowing that some of the food I ate may have come from there got my mind thinking about possibilities I had never considered before.

Not only then but throughout the entire summer trip, I concluded that the best way to learn about and appreciate one's environment was simply to see it. In most cases, seeing the living world around you leaves more of an impression than classroom instruction, photos in books, or lectures.

* * *

Around noon came a ride from a man driving a station wagon. Station wagons were as popular then as SUVs are today. Tommy and I threw our

---

[16] Arlington National Cemetery is a United States military cemetery in Arlington County, Virginia, across the Potomac River from Washington, DC, in whose 639 acres the dead of the nation's conflicts have been buried, beginning with the Civil War, as well as reinterred dead from earlier wars.
"Arlington National Cemetery" Wikipedia, last edited on 25 December 2022, https://en.wikipedia.org/wiki/Arlington_National_Cemetery last edited on 25 December 2022

knapsacks into the backseat. Tommy jumped into the front seat, and I got in the back. This arrangement of stowing our gear and seating was acceptable to the driver, who had exceptionally thick lenses mounted in his thick black eyeglass frames. My experience at that point was that looking through such lenses revealed only distorted vision.[17]

We were off. The car was comfortable, and we learned he was going at least two hundred miles west on 90, so all seemed good—except for the smell.

After our initial introductions and understanding of each other's destinations, Mr. Visionary lit a cigarette. I immediately knew the smell when we got in the station wagon—tobacco. His full, thick gray mustache had a noticeable section just below his nostrils that consisted of peculiar reddish-brown hairs. I deduced where the brown hair came from: he exhaled the cigarette smoke through his nose, making his mustache a secondary filter. After a couple of hours, I felt confident that Mr. Visionary could have qualified to be the chain-smoker poster boy.

Mr. Visionary was a likable guy who offered Tommy and me one piece of advice after another. He volunteered little-known techniques on how to get the best price for your hogs at market and the best way to achieve the ultimate in sexual satisfaction. Not that we showed any interest or asked for either.

At one point, we stopped for gas. Mr. Mustache coughed uncontrollably as he got out of the car and walked behind the gas station. He was gone for a long time. I asked Tommy, "What do you think happened to Mr. Mustache?"

"I have no idea, but this is getting a little weird," he replied. We both decided not to investigate just yet.

Fifteen minutes later, he came back to the car. Not that he had to give us an explanation, but it seemed mysterious that he had nothing to say. It would be good to breathe smoke-free air when this ride finished.

We covered a considerable distance thanks to several good rides, making it another good day.

It became clear that the two key cities in Minnesota were Minneapolis and Saint Paul. I recognized this since so many signs pointed out exits for

---

[17] On the school playground, we would inconsiderately refer to such glasses as having Coke-bottle lenses.

those destinations. One man who gave us a ride told us that more than half the population of Minnesota lived in or around the Twin Cities, the two closely located cities of Minneapolis and Saint Paul.

We passed farms and then some more farms, seeing few people on them.

Occasionally, we passed towns with stores that probably sold supplies to farm families, such as Bill's Feed & Grain, Valley Tractor Sales and Repair, or Ralph's Hay Storage. Sporadically, some towns had painted lines on the streets, indicating parking spaces, and a rare traffic light, indicating a visible population.

As we reached the southwestern section of Minnesota, the view shifted from farms to prairies—flat areas with few trees and large regions of tall, coarse grass. The prairies made me think it wouldn't have been out of the question to see Marshal Dillon galloping through on his horse, packing six guns and a Winchester .30-30 rifle slung in the rifle holster on the side of his horse.

Then we started seeing signs indicating we were approaching South Dakota.

GREAT PLACES, GREAT FACES (SOUTH DAKOTA)

As we crossed the line from Minnesota into South Dakota, we saw numerous signs for Sioux Falls.

I later learned that Sioux Falls was arguably the dead center of the continental United States, right in the middle of a scope's crosshairs. This questionable fact added up to be a benefit, at least at the time, for both businesses and residents of the Sioux Falls area. Imagine the advantage of having a national company located right in the middle of the United States. It resulted in the installation of large call centers to make and receive significant cost-sensitive long-distance phone calls.

Distribution allowed products to get anywhere in the country faster and often at a lower cost.

Time has brought many changes since 1970. The importance of the geographic location has changed due to the availability of numerous carriers providing fast delivery and air shipping. The introduction of the 800 number and numerous companies competing for customers' long-distance phone service dramatically reduced phone costs and practical worldwide communications using today's lightning-fast internet over the steadfast USPS mail.

My memory of Sioux Falls was that it was a different kind of city. In my world, New York City was a city. I didn't see any tall buildings in Sioux Falls. As expected, there were stores, shopping centers, and houses.

It seemed like a city spread over a wide area, a ghost town compared to the Big Apple.

Not long after we left Sioux Falls, I saw a small ranch house in prairie land as far as I could see. On the side of the yellow house was a fenced-in area similar to those used by dogs, but it wasn't. Inside the fencing was a lone buffalo! When I saw the buffalo, my first thought was of my old nickel coin tucked away somewhere at home.

I had seen a buffalo on display at the Museum of Natural History in New York City, but this was my first live one. While I will never know for sure, I guessed someone in that yellow house was keeping the buffalo as either a pet, future food, or, conceivably, a memento maintained by a delusional fan of the NFL Buffalo Bills football team. Scott Norwood may have single-handedly put that team on the map.[18]

* * *

As we continued heading west on Interstate 90, along the southern border of South Dakota (Nebraska was south of us the whole length of the state), we started seeing signs pointing drivers to at least seven separate Indian reservations—another thing we didn't see in New Jersey.

Somewhere in central South Dakota, a station wagon pulled over to the side of the highway to give us a ride. We noticed a unique smell when we got in the vehicle. This ride turned out to be one of the more odoriferous ones of the trip.

I noticed the hat on the man about to give us a ride. It was white, something like a lightweight cotton baseball cap. There was no team logo, but there was the name of a chain of hardware stores that had gone belly-up about a decade earlier. Then I noticed he was wearing an apron with blotches of various colors. At that point, I put it together. The giveaway

---

[18] Super Bowl XXV fans may remember this infamous placekicker ending the Bills' first ever quest for a Super Bowl win by missing a forty-seven-yard field goal kick in the remaining eight seconds of the game, handing the New York Giants the win. Two major motion pictures released after this game contained plots of a player missing a clutch kick at the end of the game. One referred to an attempt to murder a former Buffalo kicker by the name of Scott Wood, whose missed field goal led to the loss of a large bet and, subsequently, his serving a prison term when he took the fall for his bookie.

was the smell of turpentine. That, coupled with his outfit, identified him as a painter. I turned around to see the back section of the station wagon. There were stacks of paint cans, rags, paintbrushes, tarps, rollers, and other supplies critical to the trade.

We passed a sign: "Deadwood: Population 986." I mentioned something to the effect that the name Deadwood sounded western. Mr. Paint Man explained that Deadwood had come about after the Black Hills gold rush only a few years after the Civil War.[19] A miner found gold in a narrow canyon in the Northern Black Hills. The canyon became known as Deadwood Gulch because of the many dead trees that lined the canyon walls at the time.

We weren't in New Jersey anymore.

Tommy and I learned much more about different kinds of paints, including the many benefits of latex.

Mr. Paint Man let us in on a secret. Everyone knew how important it was to clean up after painting, but most people weren't aware of all the techniques. He let us in on his professional secrets. Until then, I hadn't known there was a special paint just for bathrooms and how critical it was to use it for that room. He also told us about paintbrushes. He stressed that it was crucial to use the right brush since that made the paint application smoother, and a brush could be reused many more times if cleaned correctly after each use. As his eyes focused on the roadway ahead, he said confidently, "Saving money on cheaper brushes isn't worth it." Later in life, I learned just how right he was.

Mr. Paint Man was thrilled to share his unique skill set with us while exuding the pride he'd learned through experience.

After an excellent two-hour ride, it was great, once again, to inhale some clean, fresh air. Thirty seconds later, I had forgotten most of what we learned about painting, except for a few items mentioned. *It's funny how some little things you just don't forget.*

South Dakota would catch one's attention for the signs alone; for

---

[19] Practically overnight, the tiny gold camp boomed into a town that played by its own rules. It attracted outlaws, gamblers, and gunslingers along with the gold seekers. Wild Bill Hickok was one of the men who came looking for fortune. But just a few short weeks after arriving, he was gunned down while holding a poker hand of aces and eights—forever after known as the Dead Man's Hand.

example, we saw many signs for the Missouri River and the city of Pierre. When we stopped at a rest area for a bathroom break, I read a plaque giving some background about Pierre. For example, I learned from the plaque that Pierre first had been established on the bank of the Missouri River opposite Fort Pierre and that Pierre had been the state capital since 79 AD. Don't hold me to the actual date; let's say it has been there for a long time.

Take that, geography and history classes! OK, it wouldn't get me into Harvard, but I was learning things now that I would never learn in high school. My parents might have pointed out that I didn't know these things because I lacked academic enthusiasm. They would have been right.

Our next ride was in another pickup truck. The young man driving was friendly as Tommy and I crunched into the single seat in the cab with our gear stacked on top of our laps. This ride was more challenging since this particular older pickup truck shifter extended about three feet from the floor; similar to modern-day commercial airliners, it took away some much-needed leg space.

Climbing into the truck's cab, I saw a real-life gun rack mounted behind our heads for the first time. Fortunately, there were no guns, but the rack was a good indication that they weren't far away. The gun rack showed us that we were gradually entering the western United States.

We now left central daylight time, entering mountain daylight time.

* * *

Riding on Interstate 90, we passed a vast area of land that sharply stood out. The land was barren, consisting of only rough black rock. In the distance, I saw a few flat grass areas, almost plateaus. Farther beyond were hills of bare brownish rock with nothing growing on them. Nothing could have lived there. Our driver told us it was the Badlands. *This must have been what it was like for the astronauts as they landed on the moon.* There was no evidence of life, only barren land with unusual rock formations.

I didn't realize the importance of the signs for Sturgis at the time. Later in life, I learned that countless motorcyclists met there at the Sturgis Motorcycle Rally each August. While I never made the trip, I can easily visualize what it would have been like to ride my BMW motorcycle to Sturgis for the rally. Reflecting, I wish I had.

The prominent place we missed in South Dakota was Mount

Rushmore,[20] the rock carving of four distinguished American presidents. We were close to many sights yet never saw them since the unwritten rule in our situation was to stick with your ride to get to your destination.[21]

Again, the signs pointed out the exits for famous locations we had heard about—some since grammar school. We knew those places were out there—just out of our reach. I found it amazing how many famous locations we either saw glimpses of or passed signs for. South Dakota made a rousing impression on me. It's on my bucket list to go back.

While we were on the side of the highway, waiting for the next car to stop, I said, "Say, Tommy, did you notice all the famous places we saw exit signs for?"

He said, "Yeah, it could be neat to go check some of them out."

We eventually rationalized that as much as we would have liked to visit and sightsee some of those places, it was not in our best interest. We concluded that the reduced traffic flow on roads leading to and from those sites wasn't worth the risk of getting stuck. We decided to play it safe and stick with the highway since even though we had the whole summer ahead of us, we still had a long way to go—what a mature decision.

For the first time that summer, a gentle sense arose in the back of my mind: *What happens if we are in the Midwest, or wherever, and can't make it back in time for school? How embarrassing would it be to call home and ask for help because I was stuck somewhere?* After a fragment of a second, possibly less, I dismissed the cockamamie thought from my mind for the next two months.

---

[20] Fortunately, Mount Rushmore was spared defacement during the civil unrest that occurred during the summer of 2020.

[21] This rule does not apply to drifters, but did it apply to us?

CHAPTER 10

WYOMING, FOREVER WEST

When we crossed over from South Dakota into Wyoming, we didn't know what to expect or what we might experience there. At that point in our trip, each state was becoming a unique adventure; we had no idea what to expect as we entered them—Wyoming would be no different.

When we entered Wyoming, it began to get dark, so we needed a place to sleep for the night. After seeing a sign for Black Hills National Forest, we decided to camp in the woods there, just as we had in eastern South Dakota.

As our ride let us off at the exit ramp, the sign read, "Sundance/Black Hills National Forest." Sundance stuck in my mind because I recently saw a movie called *Butch Cassidy and the Sundance Kid*.[22] The film tells the story of Wild West outlaws Robert LeRoy Parker, known as Butch Cassidy (Paul Newman), and his partner, Harry Longabaugh, a.k.a. the Sundance Kid (Robert Redford), running from a crack US posse after a string of train robberies. That year, each student in our class had been assigned to write a report about a well-known person in history. I had chosen the Sundance Kid as my person to write about, influenced by the movie. I loved the 1969 movie and wondered if this was where the Sundance Kid was from as I looked at *Sundance* posted on the exit sign. My report was about a boy of about fifteen who headed west and received his nickname when arrested for stealing a horse in Sundance, Wyoming. After a few years

---

[22] *"Butch Cassidy and the Sundance Kid," Wikipedia,* last edited on December 25, 2022,
https://en.wikipedia.org/wiki/Butch_Cassidy_and_the_Sundance_Kid.

in jail, the Sundance Kid resumed a career in crime, robbing trains and banks. He eventually met up with Butch Cassidy and became part of a gang of outlaws. My guess about the Sundance Kid being from Sundance, Wyoming, wasn't exactly correct, but it was close.

My mind and imagination drifted to wondering if Tommy Sidhad and I could be the modern-day version of those outlaw cowboys, even though we were neither outlaws nor cowboys. That thought was ridiculous—posses didn't exist anymore.

* * *

The Black Hills National Forest comprises more than a million acres of forested hills and mountains approximately 110 miles long land 70 miles wide. This national forest is in northwestern Wyoming, with even larger sections of the same parklands in South Dakota.

As we hiked into the park, we saw signs for numerous campsites, which we ignored because they cost money. We simply found an area of trees out of any park ranger's sight. After a good night's rest, we packed up and headed back toward the Interstate 90 West ramp.

* * *

I don't think it was any one particular thing or venture, but once again, I sensed that we were now Out West. This sense of regional awareness increased as we traveled from state to state, moving through time zones, and I began picking up on a cocktail of differing lifestyles and attitudes. Examples included the increased number of pickup trucks with gun-rack mounts and the fact that some of the racks now held guns. One visual that hit me was the heightened concentration of so many people in general wearing cowboy boots and hats.

About every ride we got in, the radio inevitably was on at some point. As we traveled across the country, notably, the car radios gradually, almost imperceptibly, shifted; the genre of music slowly unfolded from pop to a mix of pop and country and then eventually to all country-and-western music. The bleeding heartbreak, dog-dying grief, singing about lonely cowboy blues, and slide-guitar twang of country-and-western music had a fingernails-scratching-a-chalkboard impact on me.

The New York City Metropolitan area is comprised of about 12.5 million people, depending on whose numbers you believe. Based on my extensive familiarity with the region, I estimate that between eight and twelve individuals in this population listen to country-and-western, and even fewer would admit to it.

Enough on the subject, since I tend to identify with the Geraldo Rivera era of rock.

CHAPTER 11

JOYRIDE

We picked up a ride heading west from two teenage boys. They almost looked like identical twins with their black hair slicked back and intentionally greased. Their car was an older black four-door sedan. Tommy and I climbed into the backseat with our gear. As we got in, we found the car's floor littered with empty beer cans and four cats.

I hate cats, and why four? My allergic reaction to them didn't enhance any affection.

Hey, a ride was a ride.

After initial introductions, we asked where they were going. One responded, "No idea, and don't give a shit." All the empty beer cans on the floor might have partially explained their undetermined sense of direction. They were in a cheerful mood.

At one point ahead, a dead deer lay on the highway's shoulder. The driver swerved the car, attempting to run over it. After a jarring thumpity-bump, he maneuvered back onto the highway lane. Tommy and I were shocked at what we had just witnessed. *What the hell is happening?*

Our two teenage hosts were laughing loudly. The maneuver seemed to be the funniest thing they had done in their lifetime. Both guys laughed uncontrollably, so hard that tears began pouring down their faces. The twins' fit of sidesplitting laughter forced the passenger to double over in the front car seat, gasping for air, as his face turned red. Considering how drunk the driver was, it seemed incredible that he maintained control of the car as well as he did. *Seriously, is it possible these guys might die laughing?*

After hearing a change in the car's sound, they looked back through the rear window at the highway behind them. What they saw got them laughing even harder. They realized that running over the dead deer had caused ten feet of the muffler, along with the associated pipes, to be yanked free from the car's undercarriage; it now lay mangled on the highway.

Once again, maybe we were getting close to the Twilight Zone.

What is it with the damn cats? I noticed the cats were amusing themselves by attempting to stay balanced on the rounded beer cans scattered on the floor. Ah, perhaps the cats had been drinking beer too.

The hysteria was so severe now that I thought they would lose it completely. Obviously, they didn't have the slightest concern, financial or otherwise, that the muffler was now dislocated from the car and lying on the road. The now roaring engine noise only made the situation hilarious to the guys as the uncontrolled laughing fit continued.

While they were having a great time, Tommy and I exhibited looks of quiet concern as we pensively observed it all, finding nothing humorous.

I wondered why causing significant damage to their car was funny and not a reason to panic. It then occurred to me that possibly the vehicle wasn't their car—perhaps it was even stolen—so there was no reason for them to care.

After a Wyoming State Police car flew past with lights flashing and siren screaming, probably responding to some emergency call (perchance report of a drunk driver), the teenagers seemed to straighten up quickly. The laughter and devil-may-care attitude ended, and they now appeared alarmed. They decided to get off the highway immediately and informed us that the lift was over, suggesting we get off at the approaching exit. The exit was for Buffalo, Wyoming.

* * *

While we waited for our next ride, my mind roamed to a new popular food I had recently heard about: buffalo wings. I had never eaten them and wondered what the big deal could be over chicken wings. Years later, I would learn about them at a Hooters restaurant in New York City. I wondered if Buffalo, Wyoming, was where buffalo wings had been invented.

Wrong.

They originated in Buffalo, New York. Considering we were in Wyoming, I am now sure the town name Buffalo referenced the Wyoming regional animal.

CHAPTER 12

A GLIMPSE

Our next ride was from another guy in a pickup truck. He told us he was traveling about another two hundred miles on Interstate 90. While that sounded great, we didn't realize we were traveling in the wrong direction for many of those miles. At a certain point, we passed a sign saying, "Welcome to Montana: Big Sky Country." Tommy and I looked at each other, both wondering, *Montana?* I was naive. All I knew about Montana was that it was one of those states way out there somewhere.

Suddenly, Tommy spotted a sign indicating we were on I-90 North. True to his style, within a fragment of a second after, Tommy blurted, "North? Wait a minute!" The driver and I turned to see the widened eyes on his shocked face as he added, "Wait a second—we are supposed to be going west. Our destination is California, not Canada."

We started firing questions at the respectable man giving us a ride. Yes, we were going north into Montana. Sharing Tommy's concern, I said, "I think we should get off ASAP and hitch back in the other direction to get back on track. Something has gone wrong, because this is definitely not the direction we should be going."

The friendly pickup truck driver, hearing our dilemma, stopped to let us off, allowing us to cross the highway and start hitchhiking south on Interstate 90.

The spot where we crossed the highway in the vast state of Montana displayed a stunning country landscape. I thought that Montana indeed did have a big sky.

That sky was a picturesque deep dark blue that late afternoon. The air was remarkably crisp and clean, causing me to take a few deep breaths to absorb it. There was not a building in sight, which made the place seem untouched.

The substantial deep blue sky appeared enhanced by a backdrop of magnificent, tall mountains shooting up from the ground on either side of the skyline, reaching up into the sky. The bright green of the evergreen trees on the mountains provided a vivid contrast to the blue sky. The colors were an awesome sight! Once again, I took in deep breaths of the abundant fresh, clean air, which made the impact of this adventure even more extraordinary. I can still picture it today.

THE CARAVAN

Our first ride on the rebound took us south about ten miles, and we crossed the state line back into Wyoming. The next ride took us only a short distance before exiting the highway and dropping us off in a remote area.

When Tommy and I got out of the car, we looked at our surroundings, wondering where we were going from there. We were no longer on the interstate; we were now in a desolate area where just two small roads crossed. Somewhat confused, we walked over to the nearby gas station, the only building or sign of visible human life, and asked the single gas pump guy to recommend the best way to get back on our trail west. He pointed to a small two-lane road (nothing like Interstate 90), noting that it went west. The way he said it was less than inspiring.

We felt stuck, without any other choices. At least it kept our direction focused west, albeit on a much-less-traveled road. As expected, less traffic lowered the odds of getting a ride, and we accepted the fact that this might take some time. We would walk for a while, take a rest, and then resume walking, as there was next to no traffic, when suddenly, seemingly out of nowhere, along came a stream of slow-moving vehicles consisting of three VW Microbuses, two loaded sedans, one hearse, and two motorcycles. What were we seeing?

The ride might not have been the most memorable of the trip, but it certainly made the top ten. It made me think of what a wagon train, with horses pulling covered wagons, must have been like in the early West. The passengers in this group were primarily young people of varying ages. One of the things that made this episode of our adventure so different was that rather than a single car or pickup truck stopping, the whole caravan of vehicles stopped for us simultaneously!

I had one of those rare once-in-a-lifetime feelings that I was seeing something extraordinary happen right in front of me.

The black hearse stopped closest to us and opened the back doors, allowing Tommy and me to climb in with our gear. At least we entered it with youth and vitality and actively breathing, unlike the thousand—possibly more, considering the age of the hearse—who'd passed the same doors in a coffin. You may have a picture in mind of what a hearse looks like; however, this windowless black hearse was like a tank from the 1950s. It was solid black on the outside, of course, with a few nicks and dents, and the lack of windows gave it a tomb-like feeling.

Two long-haired, bearded guys were in the front seat, while another guy and his girlfriend, along with two other traveling drifters similar to Tommy and me, occupied the vestibule in the back of the hearse. The hearse had plenty of room, permitting all of us to be entombed comfortably.

Once we had climbed aboard, the drivers all put their vehicles in gear, and we rolled onward. Gradually, we started to meet our fellow transient excursionists. Some were families with a few young children, while most were old enough to drive; Tommy and I, other than the small children, were a couple of the youngest. They all were friendly and easy to relate to.

We learned that this roaming caravan had no specific destination and, for the most part, kept together, occasionally dropping someone off and adding others, such as Tommy and me. There were more than thirty people altogether, and we gradually got to know many of them. We were on a small road with minimal traffic, so we felt lucky to be getting this ride, with the added benefit that they were going west. After passing through a small town as it started to get dark, the caravan pulled over into a densely wooded area, where we all set up a group camp among the trees.

Some of them started cooking while four campfires burned. In northern Wyoming, where summer nights could get cold, they built fires to cook food and provide warmth.

Tommy and I sat around sharing our thoughts about this unique ride we were on. We also agreed we were hungry, noting that we didn't have food, unlike the others. Several of our new family members noticed that Tommy and I had nothing to eat, so they came over to offer us food. The food was great—hey, anything would have tasted good at that point. More important was the feeling of camaraderie. It was warm and family-like because everyone seemed to look out for one another. Groovy, baby. Just groovy.

It felt as if we were all one happy family sharing this traveling experience with one another. One couple in a VW Microbus had two young children who expressed riveting interest in running around the camp and found everything hilarious.

* * *

It was an era of peace, love, and harmony. These feelings of consciousness were usually consistent with people, mainly within a specific age range, who maintained an open way of thinking and were in a societal place to be part of the whole generational ideology. The people in this caravan were the essence of those values and times.

If you watched *Rowan & Martin's Laugh-In* (a 1960s TV comedy series) and found it funny, you might find that it gave a flavor of this era. If none of this makes sense to you, that's OK; find a rerun, and watch it sometime.

* * *

While in my sleeping bag for the night, I became suspicious that more than just sleeping was going on in the vehicles, especially the ones with curtains, because the squeaking suspensions were in rhythm with the moaning sounds of oohs and aahs.

Cleaning up our camp on a sunny morning was a careful process: everyone wanted to leave the area exactly as we'd found it, in its natural state, without a trace of refuse. Some pulled up tents. Like Tommy and I, many rolled up their sleeping bags while others organized their vehicles for another day of traveling. A few even enjoyed the luxury of brushing their teeth. Most used the bathroom—the woods—and then piled into their associated rides.

The caravan drove about a mile from the campsite to the small town we had passed the night before. The entire fleet pulled into a café parking lot for breakfast. Only a couple of customers were in the café when we arrived. Our arrival took up all the available parking spaces, forcing others to park in the street, while motorcycles easily pulled into tight spaces not necessarily designed for parking.

I realized that what we knew as a *diner* back east was referred to as a *café*. It was the same type of restaurant, merely with a different label. We noticed this more as we journeyed west; gradually, diners were completely replaced by cafés.

The few customers and waitresses must have been astonished upon seeing about thirty wandering hippies walk into the restaurant and occupy every last seat. The two girls waitressing were probably bored out of their minds until our arrival, which threw them into a frenzy of trying to keep up with the sudden onslaught of customers. The cook must have been crackerjack because he quickly managed to get all the orders out. Tommy and I figured we could spend two dollars on this meal since we hadn't used our allotted allowance the day before. It was outstanding! Amazing that you can remember how much you enjoyed a single meal so long ago. Everybody paid up, and we clambered back into the hearse and proceeded west on the tree-shaded forested road, seeing some beautiful Wyoming hills and mountains.

As we spent more time with our family of fellow transients, we got to know them better, including names, destinations, and where home was for them. Tommy and I were surprised to learn we were the farthest from home of all the group members.

The time came to part ways with the caravan when they decided to head south, while we remained concentrated on continuing west. Too bad they weren't continuing west. This adventure covered some distance, and the friendly company made it an enjoyable ride.

CHAPTER 14

YELLOWSTONE

Throughout the state of Wyoming, I noticed many signs stating, "Closed in Winter." While we were enjoying comfortable summer weather, I reckoned they must have endured some severe winter weather in that territory.

The next ride took us about fifty miles to an exit with a Burger King, where we spent our daily allotment of one dollar. We could stretch the buck to buy a burger for each of us and one order of fries to share, plus take advantage of the free water and use of the restroom facilities.

After our meal, the next ride took us about twenty-five miles to an exit a few miles before Yellowstone. We had to walk more than a mile, lugging the heavy gear, to get close to the park. We were exhausted! After finding some trees to sleep beneath, we rolled out our sleeping bags and slept well.

The following day, we continued hitchhiking west and soon saw signs for the Yellowstone National Park entrance.

The Roosevelt Arch entrance to Yellowstone National Park (iStock).

Yellowstone National Park was a place I had heard of before but knew nothing about. Rides going through that area were typically short, as they were primarily from tourists going from one area of the massive park to another. We were lucky enough to see some fantastic sights between and during these rides.

One view that stood out was seeing a geyser for the first time. Some were hot springs in which the water intermittently boiled; some sent tall columns of water and steam into the air. The nearly five hundred geysers were all over Yellowstone, with more in other parts of Wyoming.

The first geyser I saw was smaller than a pond or even a small swimming pool. The water was bubbling like a rolling boil in a pot on the stove. It was an unexpected sight to see scalding-hot water steaming, despite the warm summer day.

Another interesting fact we learned is that geysers vary significantly in temperature, ranging from warm to extremely hot. Fortunately, most geysers are within rugged rocks, a deterrent to anyone adventurous or misguided enough to go swimming—or, in this case, anyone who had the desire to be cooked like a hard-boiled egg. Of course, there were also signs forbidding swimming.

On another short ride through the park, the young couple giving us a lift slowed down to observe and take pictures of a herd of 100 to 150 buffalo on the grassland (prairie). I was amazed at the immense size of the animals, their vast number, and how fast they moved. The driver slowed to get a good look and snap a couple of photos as we got beastly close to them. I was fascinated by their powerful presence.

Again, I thought, *We're not in New Jersey anymore.*

Herd of bison in the Hayden Valley, Yellowstone National Park (JREden/iStock).

During our ride through the park, I noticed many campsites had pitched tents, including people getting familiar with their new vacation home in the great outdoors.

At one point, we saw a large cloth bag hanging from a branch near a campsite. I said, "Tommy, look at those bags hanging from the tree. What do you suppose that's all about?"

He looked puzzled and said, "I have no idea."

The couple giving us a ride overheard our curiosity and explained that many grizzly bears in the area often fed on campers' "gourmet" food. The campers dangled the food from a tree branch to keep the food out of reach from the bears. Bears could easily climb trees but often were too heavy for the branches to support them. It was supposed to be a safe place to keep their food and, most importantly, helped to avoid close encounters with aggressive, determined, hungry bears.

"Hey, Tommy, we should be fine since we don't have any food with us," I said.

He instantaneously replied, "Sure, unless they get hungry for people."

That was a concerning thought, though I doubted the National Park

Service would have allowed so many people to visit if there were any serious threats from bears.

* * *

Another young couple enjoying the magical world of Yellowstone National Park had a significant destination in mind. They wanted to see Old Faithful. Tommy and I were thrilled to join them to see it.

There was a ranger building near the Old Faithful geyser, and since we had to wait for the next time the geyser would go off (a frequently updated sign told visitors the time of the next eruption), we browsed inside a public area of the building, where we learned that Congress had established Yellowstone as America's first national park. The park's land originally came from the territories of Montana and Wyoming. Today the park, mainly in Wyoming, has smaller sections in Montana and Idaho. Yellowstone National Park consists of more than 2.2 million acres, more than the combined states of Rhode Island and Delaware. This move by Congress became known as the Act of March 1, 1872.[23]

Meeting a park ranger there, I asked him questions about Old Faithful. They were probably minor questions he had already answered more than a thousand times that summer.

Our conversation turned out to be a learning experience for me. I asked the ranger how the geyser worked and how frequently it shot the water up. He smiled at me and explained that the Old Faithful geyser was an eruption that shot vast amounts of water more than one hundred feet into the air. He also cautioned me not to get close, as the water from the geyser was extremely hot and could burn you.

I then asked him, "Why do they call it Old Faithful?"

He told Tommy and me that Native American Indian tribes had first discovered Old Faithful, possibly as far back as eleven thousand years ago. More recently, a European-led expedition had been the first group of people to come across the geyser. Like the Indians, they'd noticed that the geyser went off every eighty-eight to ninety-one minutes.

---

[23] "Learn About the Park," *National Park Service*, Last updated: September 6, 2019, https://www.nps.gov/articles/quick-nps-history.htm

Tourists gather to watch as Old Faithful geyser in Yellowstone National Park erupts, forcing out boiling water and steam from the bedrock below (iStock).

Because of its precise timing, the expedition had named the geyser Old Faithful.

He said that people from all over the world came to see Old Faithful erupt.

Earlier, when Tommy and I had been walking around the designated walkway path, which also served to limit how close you could get to the geyser, I'd noticed a sign that said, "Do Not Put Clothes in Geyser." I asked the ranger about the sign: "What does that mean?"

Again, he smiled. He said, "Back in the early 1900s, people used to throw their clothes into the geyser, and they went deep down into the ground in bubbling hot water that could get up to two hundred degrees. When the geyser erupted, out came their superclean clothes. People had never seen their clothes so clean! Unfortunately, one time, people put so many clothes into the geyser that it clogged it up, preventing the geyser from erupting for several days."

I find it interesting that while I may not remember what I had for breakfast yesterday, some memories remain clear and seem to last a lifetime. Yellowstone is one of those memories.

* * *

Yellowstone was tucked away in the northwest corner of Wyoming. Throughout the trip, we had been continuously heading west. The following state, going west, was Idaho.

"Well, I guess we'll leave the park through the west entrance and exit into Idaho. What do you think there is in Idaho?" Tommy asked.

"I'm not completely sure." The truth was, I had no idea. "Idaho doesn't seem to have any sizzle to it, but Colorado does. What do you say we check that out?"

"Yeah, sounds good," he replied.

Based on our incomplete knowledge of Idaho, we made another junior executive decision to leave Yellowstone via the south exit from the park. Taking that route would shift our westerly focus of California, directing us south, keeping us within Wyoming instead of sending us west to Idaho.

Consequently, Colorado became our next destination after our somewhat haphazard joint decision to head south. Colorado, the state south of Wyoming, sounded like a place too cool to pass up.

THE CAFÉ

About thirty miles south of Yellowstone, our ride dropped us off in a small Wyoming town. It was sizable enough to have a main street with parking spaces and a couple of traffic lights.

As I mentioned earlier, the farther we traveled, the more we found that what we knew as *diners* were called *cafés*—the similarities between the two were remarkable.

The cafés all had decor similar to the diners, including a counter where one could eat a meal sitting on a round seat that could spin. Or customers could choose a booth or table to eat their grub. The menu was mostly the same. The jukebox (younger readers, ask your parents or grandparents or prehistoric old people what a jukebox was) had identical worn 45-rpm records, albeit songs here were primarily all of the country-and-western genre.

We went into the café and took stool seats at the counter. Even the gum-chewing waitress was the same. I assumed that since we looked so out of place, she didn't refer to us as *honey*.

Most patrons watched us, staying alert to everything we said or did. Others seemed to be keeping track of us out of concern or possible fear; regardless, everyone seemed alarmed by the strangers who'd just wandered into the town café.

Tommy and I entered the café noticeably dragging since we were running on little sleep from the previous night. We must have appeared like the walking dead. We were exhausted. We walked to the counter and sat next to each other, dropping our gear onto the floor.

We decided to spend our dollar-a-day allotment at the café. We each ordered an egg with coffee. The egg plate came with two pieces of toast and hashed brown potatoes. We each enjoyed a filling meal, coffee, and complimentary water.

I was so beat that I struggled to stay awake. My head hung down as I mindlessly stared at the floor. Someone then sat on the counter stool next to me, and I noticed that the person was wearing cowboy boots. I had seen cowboy boots on TV before or on a person wearing a cowboy costume, but I had never seen anyone wearing them as usual footwear. Looking at the boots, I noticed shiny silver metal attached to the back of his bootheels. It took me a few seconds to retrieve the word: *spurs*. Yes, I calculated they must be spurs, based on TV westerns like *Bonanza, Gunsmoke, Rawhide, The Rifleman*, and others.

The sight aroused my curiosity. I had to see who this guy was.

As I elevated my vision, I saw, attached to his blue jeans, a holster with a six-gun. The bottom of the holster had a leather strap wrapped around his thigh. I guessed the strap was to keep the gun holster securely in place, or perhaps it helped support a quick draw.

We were far away from New Jersey now!

I wanted to talk with the guy to understand why he wore that attire. Then I noticed the silver star on his chest, attached to his plaid shirt. That explained it all. When I looked at his face, he was staring directly at me. That was when I noticed the cowboy hat on his head. I knew we were in Wyoming, but it felt like we were in a saloon in Benson, Arizona, just outside Tombstone. For a tiny space in time, I thought I was being beamed back to the 1880s.

Even though I was only sixteen, I'd had my share of interfaces with law enforcement, but I never had met an officer resembling the town sheriff. I was amused at the man's attire and came close to the beginning of a laugh, but the intelligent part of me managed to keep a controlled straight face. After all, despite his appearance, he was a cop.

The sheriff didn't waste any time in getting started with his questions. He asked, "Where are you boys coming from? What are you doing here? Where are you going? How are you going to get there? Where do you sleep?" Part of the questioning included his request for each of our IDs. Many of his questions were the same ones my parents had asked me when I told them I wanted to go on this adventure. He wanted a good understanding of these two young strangers and what they were doing in his town.

After learning who we were and our situation, he eased up as we answered all his questions, maybe partly because he realized we were only passing through and would be leaving town after our minuscule breakfast. He likely concluded we weren't a threat to the community, and his attitude changed from an investigative concern to an admiration of our determination.

As we talked, he seemed less concerned that we could be troublemakers, and his questions now stemmed from curiosity.

At that point, he told us, "So far this summer, three other longhairs like yourselves were found fatally shot on the sides of roads in Wyoming." He was concerned enough to say, "Seriously, be very careful."

I took his words as genuine and thought he liked us enough to share this particular alert.

I realized he had never ordered anything, and no waitress had offered to take his order. We were getting checked out. Coincidentally, when the sheriff got up to leave, our waitress arrived to refill the coffees we'd requested before we met with the sheriff. The ten-minute intervention once again made me feel as if we'd entered the Wild West.

After we finished our coffee (after numerous refills) and took a much-needed bathroom break, we collected our gear and headed out the café door onto the sidewalk. A young boy, approximately six or seven years old, stood with his mother, waiting to cross the street safely. The boy turned around, saw us, and yelled, "Mama, look at those men with long hair!" It got the mother's attention, and she looked toward us and immediately grabbed her son's arm, yanking him away from us as quickly as possible.

It was time to saddle up and mosey out of town.

CHAPTER 16

WYOMING GRAND TETONS

Our encounter at the café occurred in a small town on the hundred-mile stretch between Yellowstone's south entrance and exit and a town called Jackson Hole. It seemed minutes after the café, a stunning sight came into view: the Grand Tetons. The Grand Teton mountain range runs north and south for about forty miles.

The reflections of the Grand Teton mountain in Grand Teton National Park (iStock).

At that point, the road we were on took us south, right along the base of the impressive mountain range. The Grand Tetons seemed to jut sharply into the sky from the base-level ground we were on. It was the middle of summer, yet some of the peaks were snow-covered.

What a breathtaking sight! At the time, I couldn't begin to know how long the picture of seeing that site would remain in my brain.

Looking out the car window, we remained fixated on the Grand Teton range's majestic beauty. I thought there was no way I, or anyone, could have climbed that steep mountain—wrong. I later learned that many people did climb that magnificent mountain range.

The Grand Tetons penetrated my sense of sight through their natural beauty and the aroma in the air from the pine and evergreen trees.

While we looked out the car window at the picturesque Grand Tetons, the driver slowed down to see why many cars suddenly had stopped ahead of us. The cars parked on the sides of the road belonged to a crowd looking at something. The young couple giving us the ride also pulled over to check it out.

The attraction was the National Elk Refuge. The refuge is across the street from the base of the Grand Tetons (the two parks are connected).[24] The newly established National Park Service set up the National Elk Refuge in the early 1900s to protect the animals' habitat. Most notably, the refuge provides sanctuary for the large elk population and other wildlife that came close to extinction at one point.

We crossed the street to see a large group of people standing and looking at a field larger than four football fields. What immediately stood out were hundreds—maybe more than hundreds—of dull whitish-gray antlers lying on the ground. Some people had used many antlers to build an archway approximately twenty feet high and large enough to drive a car through.

The sign told us that elk were part of the deer family, only larger and heavier animals. Like deer, only the males had antlers. The male elk's antlers started growing each spring and were shed months later that winter. Elk antlers could grow up to an inch per day; they were among the

---

[24] According to the National Wildlife Refuge System, within the US Fish and Wildlife Service, they manage a national network of lands and waters set aside to conserve America's fish, wildlife, and plants.

fastest-growing animal tissue on the planet.[25] I must share my observation of the US National Parks Service. Like millions of other Americans, I appreciate the great and wise decision to preserve the breathtaking natural beauty in the United States.

It may seem small, but I have always appreciated the informative signs that share the same unique design throughout America's national parks, each furnishing general information about each park's history and evolution.

I find our national parks fascinating attractions highlighting our country's natural beauty. I find it shocking that the same government that wisely created and developed the US national parks could also spend $640 on gold toilet seats in Washington, DC.[26]

* * *

After absorbing the visual impact of the National Elk Refuge, we jumped back in the car and continued south. We soon approached the town of Jackson Hole. Although I had never heard of it before, later in life, I learned it is a major tourist destination famous for its picturesque landscapes, luxury homes of celebrities, and impressive skiing—the Beverly Hills of Wyoming.

One of my key memories of Jackson Hole is the many log cabins in and around the town. The beautiful upscale log cabins were complete with impressive coordinated landscaping.[27] Another memory that stuck with me was the considerable number of ski slopes visible from almost all areas of town we passed through. The ski slopes stood out like veins weaving among the steep mountain.[28]

I didn't know that Jackson Hole was home to big-time movie stars and powerful politicians on the national level. Reflecting on what I saw then, I now understand why this town might attract high-profile people.

---

[25] According to the National Wildlife Refuge System, within the US Fish and Wildlife Service, they manage a national network of lands and waters set aside to conserve America's fish, wildlife, and plants.

[26] Perhaps the most memorable depiction of the problem was a cartoon by the *Washington Post*'s Herb Block that showed Reagan, with Secretary of Defense Caspar Weinberger, wearing the $640 toilet seat around his neck.

[27] I didn't see any front lawns with abandoned, rusted-out cars sitting on blocks; broken washing machines; or retired refrigerators.

[28] These trails were the only spots on the mountain missing trees.

DECIDING WHICH WAY TO GO

In review, we entered Wyoming in the northeast corner, crossing the state to Yellowstone National Park in the extreme northwest corner of the state. We exited Yellowstone through the southern gate, proceeding directly south. This route put us on a direct path to Grand Teton National Park, the National Elk Refuge, and Jackson Hole.

At that point, Tommy and I needed to decide where and how to get to Colorado from there. While we stood on the side of the road, waiting for our next ride, Tommy asked, "How are we going to get to Colorado? I mean, what road should we hitch to get there?"

Not even remotely aware of where we were, I replied, "Man, I have no idea."

Our next ride stopped to gas up, and we took the opportunity to get out and ask the attendant for a paper map of Wyoming.

"We don't give out maps, but I'll let you take a look at one," the attendant said kindly but possessively. He opened the map on the counter, allowing us to glance at it while ensuring it didn't leave his sight. It was obviously used by the gas station personnel since there were many marks on the map, including mechanics' trademark black grease from working hands.

I couldn't help but notice that he kept his suspicious eyes on us as if we were potential thieves who might steal his map.[29] OK, we weren't some clean-cut tourists, but did we look that dastardly?

For hitchhikers, leaving a ride waiting was a mortal sin, which added pressure to get our directions determined as fast as possible.

With only seconds to spare, we saw that Colorado was south of us. We made a couple of mental notes of route numbers to get us going toward Denver, Colorado, our new short-term destination. The map showed us the way to Denver would have us go back east for a good part of the day—the opposite direction we'd been traveling all summer. Traveling about a hundred miles east would allow us to catch the I-25 interstate south to Colorado. Off we went, traveling east on our way to I-25 South.

Armed with this new information, we bolted back to the shoulder of the road to avoid missing a potential ride.

---

[29] Since this was decades prior to GPS, paper maps were the only real option for road navigation assistance. Most service stations around that time were happy to provide maps gratis, along with checking the engine's oil level, checking the tire pressure, and giving out free air, as added services encouraged customers to come back. My personal observation was this: those pumping gas tended to be more focused on the job since they were not distracted on cell phones (which had not yet been invented) and seemed to be English-speaking Americans as opposed to foreign nationals.

ON THE RESERVATION

While on the way to I-25, we drove through an Indian reservation. We passed a miniature billboard that read, "Hot Springs Bath."

"Hey, Tommy, I'm not sure what you are thinking, but I could really use a bath about now," I said. A quick decision was needed, or we would soon pass the bath place.

He replied, "Yeah, sounds like a good idea. I could use a bath too." Our decision was made: we would check out the place.

There was a two-dollar charge for a bath—more than our daily allowance. However, Tommy and I had done an excellent job in managing our meager finances so far, so we agreed to splurge and treat ourselves. Besides, bathing was becoming a bona fide need. Could it have been that the last time I'd showered had been before we left New Jersey about a month ago? We weren't sure, having never been to a hot spring before, if the experience would equate to a shower, but hey, it couldn't hurt.

After we paid the man, he led us into the locker room. The locker was slightly larger than a dozen shoe boxes, so we put our clothes inside it and left our knapsacks and sleeping bags on the floor. Since it appeared no one else was there, it seemed safe. We didn't have bathing suits[30] when we decided on the hot springs bath. We never considered how that part would work.

Despite being comfortable with nudity, I did not go into the springs

---

[30] My mother initially suggested I bring one.

naked.[31] Despite our mature outlook on the subject, we went in wearing our underwear.

Then we saw a signpost reminding bathers of the following:

- o No soap, shampoo, or cleansing product is allowed. (We didn't have any, so that was no problem.)
- o Nude bathers are subject to immediate ejection.
- o No sex of any kind is permitted. (The "any kind" part screamed that they had experiences with this one.)
- o No objects are allowed in the springs.
- o No glass.

We had no problem with the rules.

The spring (actually a warm water geyser) had an irregular shape with an estimated circumference of about fifteen feet, with what appeared to be pebble clusters of brown rock. I had never seen anything like it before.

The depth varied every foot or so, and there was no visible bottom in some areas. After visual inspection, we saw that you could step into the spring water onto some solid, rough rock. Wow, it turned out to be critical to wear shorts or some other covering; otherwise, sitting on the rough rock would have aggravated one's derriere, causing one's ass to bleed.

Now we understood why no one else was there. Think about it— how many people liked having bleeding bottoms or, for frequent visitors, calluses on their tushes?

We eased into the geyser water and sat on the rocks. The water was a little more than waist-high; we sat on the rock, letting our feet dangle into the possibly bottomless water. *I never thought sitting could be this painful.*

After all we had seen in Yellowstone, we knew this was only one of the numerous types of geysers. Like seltzer water, the springs were bubbling warm water. It felt great but offered little compared to a shower. If only the rocks hadn't been so coarse on our tender young keisters. Leaving the hot springs bath, I thought that the expression "pain in the ass" had taken on a whole new meaning.

---

[31] Notwithstanding objections from the fashion industry, though no one has ever been interested in my personal views, my feeling about clothing has always been that if it's not needed for protection from the elements, it is therefore, naturally, optional.

Hoping our cheeks healed rapidly, off we went with sore rear ends, hitting the road, going east on Route 26, which would eventually take us to I-25 South.

Fifty years later, I imagine that hot springs bath is now a casino, assuredly more profitable and attracting larger crowds.

CHEYENNE

Since day one, we had been following road signs for Route XX West, so now, taking Route 26 East just seemed wrong.

Tommy and I both wanted to take our wagon train to Colorado. Our game plan was to take Route 26 East through central Wyoming, aiming for I-25 to take us directly south into Colorado.

We covered some ground that day, thanks to lassoing some good rides. Our last ride dropped us off in Cheyenne, Wyoming. We probably should have been wearing ten-gallon cowboy hats to fit in with the culture; plus, it would have helped to partially block the glare from the sun, which was starting to set.

Now it was time to figure out how and where we would find sleeping accommodations; there was not enough time to look for a place where we could get ammo for our six guns—if we'd had any.

Considering our limited budget, after splurging on the hot springs that morning, finding a free place to sleep was our next hurdle.

We started exploring Cheyenne, which didn't seem that big since it was a large area with no tall buildings. Since the signs proudly made it clear that Cheyenne was the capital of Wyoming, I expected bigger. Possibly, I was mentally comparing Cheyenne to other cities, such as New York City, the city near where I had grown up.

Tommy and I were walking around investigating the town, when we saw a long and narrow single-story brick building with a well cared for lawn and plenty of windows. "You know, it kinda looks like a school dormitory," Tommy said.

"Yeah, maybe it's a college dorm, something like the frat house we stayed at our first night out," I said.

There didn't appear to be any activity there, so we decided to check it out. I knocked on the door, and after getting no response, I reached out and twisted the knob, and voilà—the door opened. We looked at each other, somewhat surprised that it wasn't locked. No name on the building or area hinted at whom the place belonged to.

"Um, let's go check it out," Tommy said. So we did.

The Dormitory

We saw a long hallway that ran the length of the building, with doors on either side of the hallway. We walked down the hallway to one of the open doors and looked inside to scope out the room. The place was quiet and appeared empty. We didn't see or hear any signs of life.

Cautiously quiet, we slowly walked in to see what kind of place this was. There wasn't a sound in the building. We continued down the long hallway and found spacious rooms on either side of the hallway. Each room was identical, having two bunk beds with mattresses. Other than the beds, there was no furniture in them. The walls of the cinder-block structure were a shade of green similar to that of most government buildings. Everything looked comfortable and immaculately clean.

The place remained silent as we gradually walked farther into the building.

It finally started to sink in that we were in an empty dormitory. *This dorm could be an excellent find*, I thought. *Did we just hit the lottery or what?*

But it got better.

About halfway down the hallway, we came across a laundry room with several washers and dryers, all looking reasonably modern. I would not classify myself as remotely knowledgeable about how to operate a washing machine, but I recognized our need for one.[32]

"Tommy, do you know how to work a washer?"

---

[32] At that point, we were wearing some seriously dirty clothes. When they were certifiably filthy, we just stuffed them down deeper into our knapsacks.

He said, "Yeah, sure," easing my anticipated washing machine inadequacies.

To top it off, open boxes of detergent were on a shelf.

Then it got even better.

Midway through the hallway, we came across another room more extensive than the laundry room. It was a massive bathroom with many showers, toilets, and six or seven sinks with an extended mirror, enhanced by abandoned soap, shampoo, and conditioner.

"Wow, this is one neat place. It's got everything except food!" Tommy said excitedly.

I agreed. "Hey, we could use the washing machines, dryers, and showers big-time. What a great find this could be." I was still somewhat wary that it could be too good to be true. How long would this building remain empty?

Considering the current condition of our clothes and lack of bathing, we felt this was akin to discovering gold!

* * *

Walking through the building, we noticed no indication of which group of people or organization stayed here now or previously. Tommy and I considered it a mystery. The residents seemed to have gone out of their way to ensure not a shred of paper was left behind. Like in a cop-show crime scene, the location had been wiped clean, as they say.

We picked a room where each of us had our own bunk bed. We threw our knapsacks onto an available bed and rolled out our sleeping bags on soft, clean, comfortable mattresses. Stretching out on our new beds, we relaxed for a few luxurious minutes. There was a growing feeling of comfort occupying the remarkably quiet building free from typical city noises, such as traffic, honking horns, and sirens.

Looking carefully at our new surroundings, I told Tommy, "Boy, it would be great if we could spend the night here. This palace has everything. Man, I hope I have the chance to use a shower."

He quickly agreed but with a slightly different priority, saying, "Maybe now it's time to take advantage of the laundry room."

"OK. It's a gamble if we get caught, but let's do it," I said.

We lugged our knapsacks off the beds and hauled them into the laundry room. I had to give Tommy credit. He had a much better sense of how to work the machines than I did. We loaded both washing machines to get started and then "borrowed" the required detergent. Upon getting washers running, Tommy said, "Man, these machines are goin' to get a real workout."

Now we recognized that it was time to make the most of the showers pronto while we had the chance. This place was huge. There must have been six showers. There was even a large pile of clean white towels neatly stacked in the corner of the room.

We took advantage of the showers, utilizing massive amounts of soap to take on the all-important goal of getting clean. I realized how filthy my hair had become, so I shampooed it more than once. It may have been the first time I experimented with a hair conditioner. *Not bad.* It seemed to give my now longer hair a smooth kind of feel. *Interesting.* The conditioner did leave me smelling like an unmanly flower garden, but that was no problem. At least I felt clean.

We went to the laundry room with towels wrapped around us. The washing machines had finished. The wet clothes went into the dryers.[33]

We repeated the laundry process until all our clothes were surgically clean. With all the clothes washed, dried, and folded, we repacked them in our knapsacks with organized care like the treasures they had become.

We still had not heard a peep from anyone. We were growing more comfortable with the place.

Stripping down to our skivvies, a.k.a. pajamas, we called it a night. With the lights out, the only talk was about how hungry we were and the critical need for food the following day. Food was the one thing missing from this place.

We drifted off into la-la land with not even the remotest idea of what tomorrow would bring.

* * *

We woke up the following day to feel the craving ache of hunger. Hence, we decided that eating something was at the top of today's list.

---

[33] We had to wash several items twice, and a couple of items we considered unwashable and disposed of.

It may sound odd, and I didn't know Tommy's thoughts, but I was excited (almost like starting the first of school) about getting dressed in my now clean clothes.

With our knapsacks packed and sleeping bags rolled and secured to our knapsacks, we started leaving the building to see where we could get some chow. We were walking down the hallway, refreshed and now looking good in our clean clothes, toward the door to exit when we heard, "Hey, you kids—stop right there!" We turned quickly to see a cop. Since no one else was in the building, we knew he was talking to us.

Oh shit. I sensed that a problem was about to begin. I felt guilty. We probably were trespassing and had no right to be there.

"What are you kids doing in here?"

"Howdy, Officer," I said without cracking a smile at my use of the word *howdy.* "We were looking for a friend and thought this was his building, but we now realize it was the wrong one. So we're leaving now." I spoke politely. I felt some relief that I answered before Tommy since his answer to the cop would have sounded something like, "Go fuck yourself."

After getting a better look at the cop, I realized he wasn't even a real cop but a rent-a-cop or security guard.

He had us wait, standing in the hallway, while he took a quick inspection of some rooms. After a satisfactory survey, he let us go.

I blew the lingering smoke off the barrel of my six-gun. We'd dodged a bullet.

Everything is in the timing.

"Boy, that cop really scared me at first," I said.

Somewhat puzzled, Tommy said, "I doubt he could have done anything anyway. I wonder what that place is all about and, hey, why the doors were left open, especially if you need to have a fake cop occasionally check up on it. Man, it all seems a little weird."

We found a small café nearby and, for $1.25, bought an egg and bacon plate and a cup of coffee. It felt satisfying, not like we were having our last meal or anything.

We left the café, now shooting for the Colorado state line, only thirty miles south of Cheyenne, Wyoming.

THE PEARLY GATES

We left Cheyenne on a two-lane road that took us back onto I-25, heading south toward Colorado.

I will never forget the car that stopped for us on the outskirts of Cheyenne: a two-door Chevy Nova. It was a dull shade of green, with a few dents and rust spots, indicating a possible lack of care and some age, void of any polish or shine. Two men in the front seat were, appropriately, wearing sunglasses. Both men were in their thirties with beards and sunglasses similar to those of the ZZ Top band members. The unkempt, long-hanging beards weren't the only reason this ride made such an impression. The ride itself was, let's say, memorable.

Since it was a two-door model car, the passenger had to get out so we could climb into the backseat. We ended up there with all our gear sitting on our laps. The passenger returned to his seat, and off we went.

As customary, whenever we got into a vehicle that stopped to give us a ride, we asked where they were going after some pleasantries. We could then gauge how far they might be taking us, which could easily vary from two to two hundred miles.

One unique aspect of this ride was different. There were no pleasantries, and when we asked them where they were going, they said nothing—there was dead silence. Tommy and I looked at each other, bewildered at getting zero response. It was strange; that had never happened before. We didn't know what to make of it.

They were going in our direction, so Tommy and I sat back and chatted; our conversation was mostly about our lodging the night before, how good the café breakfast had been, and how nice it had been to shower and wear clean clothes.

As we left Cheyenne, the environment changed quickly from a larger town or city to desert. Yes, a real desert with nothing but sand and cacti.

Another sight you don't see in New Jersey.

It had been a good ten minutes, and the driver and passenger still had not spoken a word.

The passenger reached underneath his seat and pulled something out. I thought I caught a glint of light off metal. It got my attention, and I leaned my head forward to get a good look. *Oh shit, a handgun!* My eyes bulged. Seriously, it was an authentic revolver with a long barrel. I glanced at Tommy, whose face showed the same concern I had. *What the hell is this all about?* Then the passenger again reached underneath his seat, pulling out a box. I instantly knew it contained bullets.

He picked up the gun, popped open the chamber, pulled bullets from the box one by one, and inserted them into the gun. He did this six times, until the gun was fully loaded. He then snapped the chamber shut, returned the box of bullets underneath his seat, and placed the loaded gun on the bench-type front seat between himself and the driver.

I felt a rush of adrenaline as my mind raced with possible scenarios—none of them good—as our concerned eyes stayed laser-focused on the gun.

The sheriff's words of warning shot through my brain: "Three longhairs have been found dead on the sides of Wyoming roads this summer."

Shit, we are still in Wyoming!

There still had not been one word of communication between the two men themselves or to us.

Tommy and I became silent and looked at each other with grave anxiety. His face, I'm sure, resembled mine—not quite afraid of losing bowel control but close to it.

Without Tommy and me talking, the car became stone-cold quiet. The only sounds came from the tires rolling over the road, the breeze running through the windows, and the minimal engine noise.

As tough as I am, I was getting nervous—not very becoming of a macho boy like myself, almost impossible even to imagine.

Everything was quiet for a couple of minutes until the driver reached underneath his front seat and pulled out a double-barrel shotgun. The barrel length seemed shorter than the rifles I had seen before. I knew guns could be deadly, but in my mind, this one was indisputably a serious gun.

He put the rifle between his legs, with one end on the floor and the barrel facing the roof. Like the passenger loading the pistol, he reached under his seat and pulled out a slightly larger box filled with shotgun shells. With skill you can only gain from experience, he picked up the shotgun with one hand and snapped open the barrel. One by one, he loaded shells into the gun while using his legs to keep the gun stationary. His eyes remained focused on the road. This wasn't his first time loading a gun while driving.

After snapping the gun shut, he put the gun on the front seat between himself and the passenger. Now each of them had a loaded gun!

My mind rocketed from concern to being scared shitless and everywhere in between. Beads of sweat formed on my forehead. My heart thumped. I could feel it.

The fun was gone.

CHAPTER 21

FIGHT OR FLIGHT

I knew there was a good chance we would die soon, but I would not go easily. I would fight or do whatever it took to survive. I thought to myself, *Stop. Think.* Calming down was out of the question. *Make some sense of this. Conclusion: make a plan—fast!*

First, I was NOT going to get shot to death in the backseat of a Chevy Nova in the Wyoming desert—if I could help it.

For a millisecond, I had a vision of a few Wyoming state cops standing on the side of the road, viewing the bodies of two teenage boys lying on the side of the road, dead with fatal gunshot wounds. Not a pretty picture.

I had no idea what Tommy was thinking, but hey, *I* wasn't going to die. The perceived threat to my life started my fight-or-flight response.

Step one of my plan was to attack the two gunmen, knock them both unconscious, disable their guns, and fight for my life from there.

Then I realized I wasn't going anywhere with the heavy, bulky knapsack and sleeping bag on my lap. I was not even able to reach the front seat. It was not that the gear was so heavy, but I had no leverage in a sitting position. *Flush that plan.* The fight part wasn't looking too good.

Second, if I couldn't attack, I had to find some way to escape the car. As a last resort, I decided to jump out of the backseat car window. Sure, I would end up hurt when hitting the pavement after jumping from a car going sixty-five miles per hour, but at least there was a chance I'd survive the injuries. Alternatively, getting pumped with bullets at point-blank range offered little to no chance of survival.

I put my plan into action. Attempting to avoid suspicion, I *slowly* and cautiously started to lower the partially open backseat window, turning the handle in a circular motion.[34] The car did not have power windows, which, at the time, were a feature included only in some new deluxe, optional auto packages.

While lowering the window, my hands were getting clammy.

It is stunning how you can distinctly remember some trivial, seemingly insignificant events that happened long ago. My hands being sticky at that point is one of those distinct memories.

Damn, this back window is small. Just pushing my knapsack out of the way and climbing through the window will take some doing.

Hell, it might have been impossible to climb through, but there was no way I would give up. My mind was made up. I was determined.

Good. No one seems to notice that the back window is slowly going down.

When I decided to escape through the car window, I thought it best to keep looking straight ahead instead of watching how the window was going. Shock hit me when, while I turned the crank a little more, watching carefully, suddenly, it stopped altogether. *Shit!* It was one of those back windows that only went halfway down and came to a dead halt. My face must have been the definition of hopeless despair with a sprinkle of anger.

Several times during my window-escape phase, I glanced over to see Tommy, who appeared to be in a catatonic state.

Now the flight part wasn't working. My plans were exhausted. Panic was starting to set in.

Then it hit me, my last resort: communication. I always felt sure of my ability to talk and read people. Still, neither of our hosts had spoken a word, so there was not much to read them by; regardless, I decided to try it. I was not sure why it seemed such an obstacle; it had never been a problem before. *How do I start this conversation? What do I say? What do we have in common to help get something started?* I racked my brain for an opening line. One came to me. As far as I was concerned, the guns were the nine-hundred-pound gorilla in the car. *Here it goes.*

"Say, uh, are you guys goin' huntin'?" I stuttered.[35] *What could you*

---

[34] Note to younger readers that in 1970, most car windows were raised and closed by manually cranking a handle.

[35] My mother, a speech therapist, would have been disappointed in my pronunciation.

possibly hunt for here—cactus? Is that the best I can come up with? Hopefully, it's enough to get a conversation started.

After what seemed like a long moment, the passenger turned toward the backseat and said, "Yep." He paused. "We're going after jackrabbits." He spoke in a deep voice with a slow Texas drawl. I was amazed.

Tommy and I were in shocked silence, speechless, unable to give any response as we absorbed this new information.

There was no threat in his tone or demeanor at all. I took a deep breath and leaned a little farther back in my seat. I marveled that the only words the two guys ever uttered for the whole trip were the few words spoken by the passenger. Strange.

The adrenaline started to ease off, allowing my heart rate to normalize, until—

About five minutes later, the car slowed down, pulling over to the side of the road, onto hardened sand in the middle of an empty desert. Suddenly, I became alarmed again.

What's going on now? Why stop in the middle of nowhere?

The guns remained on the seat, and they had me concerned even more so now that we'd made this unexpected stop.

All summer, without exception, each ride dropped us off at a place near an exit ramp—in a town, at a gas station, or at an intersection—but never in the middle of nowhere. As far as the eye could see, there were only sand and cacti—no one around for miles.

Oh shit, here it comes. We are sitting ducks.

The passenger opened his car door, allowing Tommy and me to exit, giving us the chance to extend our customary "Thank you" to these scary dudes.

Of course, they wouldn't execute us in their car; they'd wait until we were out, not to leave any trace of the blood-splattered, deadly deed!

As the passenger got back in the car and shut the door, I was relieved to see that the two guns were still lying on the car's front seat.

Instead of driving back onto the road, the Chevy Nova took a sharp turn into the desert. Maybe it was some type of dirt or sand road. I watched the car drive off the road into the desert until the dust raised by the tires was no longer visible.

"I don't think I have ever been so scared. I was sure we were going to die," I said.

Tommy said nothing—he was in shock.

For a space in time,[36] I was sure we had reached the end of the line. The ordeal brought us a little closer to knockin' on heaven's door.[37]

It took me some time to understand that I had just experienced the powerful opposing emotions of living and dying. The emotions traveled at light speed from one extreme to the other within a short period of time. I was thrilled to be on the living side, still breathing. I knew we had come close to buying the farm.

Without disappointment, I prayed for deliverance and now assumed I would miss my meeting at the pearly gates with Saint Peter, at least for today—some eerie thinking for a sixteen-year-old.

I guess the Big Cheese gave us a pass today. We almost saw the Bright Shining Light. Judgment Day will have to wait for another time.

Hallelujah, we were alive!

---

[36] *Space in Time* is the name of an album by British blues-rock band Ten Years After. *Space in Time* was their sixth studio album that included songs written and performed by Alvin Lee. The album release date was August 1971, on the Chrysalis and Columbia labels.

[37] "Knockin' on Heaven's Door" is a song that was written and performed by Bob Dylan for the soundtrack of the 1973 western film drama *Pat Garrett and Billy the Kid.* Released as a single two months after the film's premiere, it became a worldwide hit, reaching the top ten in several countries.

CHAPTER 22

DENVER

Still in Wyoming, we finally got back onto I-25 and continued south. We noticed many Denver signs, which assured us that we were on the right track for our next destination.

Denver's nickname, the Mile-High City, originates from its elevation above sea level. Another less recognized definition of *mile high* refers to a self-induced high having nothing to do with sea level and everything to do with weed. Colorado's early adoption of legalizing recreational marijuana use made it one of the first states to do so. It was forty-two years after our trip (2012) when Colorado voters approved and moved forward with this radical new legalization. Of course, we were ahead of our time.

I would be remiss to leave out the other mile-high group of lovemakers who compose the Mile-High Club. This group's exclusive members are most active while traveling in larger public jet aircraft, typically more than thirty thousand feet above the ground.

We met our goal of reaching Denver, with the last ride dropping us off at night in a seedy (that's an overly generous description) section of the city. It was already dark when we arrived in town, and we didn't see a place in that city environment to roll out our sleeping bags for the night.

Maybe the gun episode from that morning made us conscious of our heightened desire to continue living.

I thought the neighborhood contained all the warning signs of drugs, gangs, knives, thieves, guns, and even the dreaded pickpockets. As poor vagrants, we fit right in.

That night would turn out to be vastly different from the previous night in the dormitory.

Since it was already late, we decided to postpone sightseeing (not that there was anything there to see) and instead find a place to crash for the night. Walking along the sidewalk, we asked the people who appeared less likely to pull out a gun if they had any suggestions where two vagabonds might find a place to sleep for the night.

Eventually, a homeless man, stinking of an attractive urine-and-wine combination, told us, "There's a brown church a couple blocks up the street. I sometimes stay there." Since we qualified as homeless, we went looking for the brown church. We found the church and opened the front door. We walked inside to find it completely dark and dead quiet, with no one in the place.[38] It was late, and we were tired, so we rolled out our sleeping bags in the aisle, on wooden floorboards. We stowed our gear between pews to hide it.

God was the only one who knew exactly who or what might wander in the church at night. We drifted off to a night of interrupted sleep.

* * *

I scratched my nose in a haze of sleep during the night and quickly returned to dreamland. A little while later, I awakened to the feeling that something light was crawling on my face. Whatever it was, I brushed it off my face and eased back to sleep. Not long after, I felt a sensation of bugs crawling on my face again. *What the hell?* Once more, I brushed whatever they were off my face without any problem. This time, I was awake.

There was enough light coming in from the streetlight outside that I could make out a bunch of long dark bugs with many legs moving around. I suddenly realized I knew what they were. *Oh, how ghastly—cockroaches crawling all over me!* They were everywhere. The church was infested with them.

Neither the Boy Scouts nor my naive suburban upbringing had prepared me for this. Other than on TV, I had never seen a cockroach before. I didn't know for sure, but I associated them with filth, the spread

---

[38] Possibly someone forgot to pay the electric bill.

of diseases, and possibly even death. Tommy appeared to be sleeping fine, but I wasn't, and I couldn't let this continue.

What do I do?

A door at the side of the church was barely visible due to the minimal light coming through the old stained-glass windows. I decided to check it out, hoping there would be a safer room free of cockroaches. Cockroaches gave me the same heebie-jeebies that snakes did—the farther away from them I was, the better.

I opened the door only to discover that it led outside the church to an alleyway. The cement alley walkway allowed about six feet between the church and another building. Although it was dark, I could see the alley littered with assorted garbage cans, broken glass, and scattered trash.

Hey, I didn't see any cockroaches.

I returned to the church, retrieved my sleeping bag, and rolled it out on the cement. I buried myself deep into my sleeping bag and then took in my night's sleep without incident.

Waking up in the morning was a happening in itself. Maybe the traffic noise from cars, buses, or sirens woke me from my cocoon. As I stuck my head out of the sleeping bag, I asked myself, *Where the hell am I? Why am I lying on the ground here?*

One of my first sights was looking through the alleyway at the busy sidewalk, seeing the traffic on the now busy street, and realizing I was sandwiched between two old buildings. On one side was the church, and on the other was an old, tall brick apartment building. Since it had been so dark in the alley, I hadn't realized the apartment building was there last night.

Last night started coming back to me. I remembered the church, the cockroaches, and my escape into the alley.

Now seeing my environment, I was amazed at the new surroundings. I sat in my sleeping bag, looking around, soaking it all in like a sponge. After putting the pieces of last night together, I returned to the church, using the same door I'd used to leave the church last night, to see Tommy sleeping just fine.

"Those cockroaches were too much for me last night, so I slept in the alley," I told Tommy when he awoke.

He gave me a puzzled look. "What cockroaches? What alley?"

BOULDER, COLORADO

Walking from the church to a moderately better section of Denver that morning, we spoke with several kids about our age. We were often told, "The place to go is Boulder." The more we heard about it, the more it sounded like a town we needed to check out. One guy a few years older than we were said, "You guys should know that Boulder is often referred to as the 'mile-higher-than-Denver town.'" Once again, he wasn't referring to the altitude!

"If this Boulder is a place we're passing anyway, let's at least check it out," I said.

"Think we'd be crazy not to. It sounds like a really cool place," Tommy said. Once again, our destination for the day, week, or month had been decided.

Since it was a Sunday, I made my weekly call home from a public phone booth. I never missed a Sunday call to tell my parents where I was, which reassured them that I was alive.

Boulder is about twenty-five miles northwest of Denver, located at the foothills of the Rocky Mountains. We exited our ride to see a spectacular sight when we arrived in Boulder. In Boulder, you can see the green Rocky Mountains climbing into the sky. You literally needed to lean your head back to see it all. At the same time, you will see homes scattered in spots among trees on the steep slopes. Tommy and I spent a few minutes just gawking at the natural beauty of the towering mountains.

Boulder is home to the main campus of the University of Colorado, the state's largest university. Its thirty thousand students make it an authentic college town. Almost every person we met there was pleasant, helpful, and friendly. We got along fine with everyone and started meeting new friends. We often walked over to groups of college students and, in a friendly way, asked questions about Boulder, including, "Can you recommend a spot where we could camp for the night? Is there a Burger King or McDonald's around here?" One such conversation with students led to an invitation to visit their home—a house they rented near the campus.

Our new friends told us that a group of about eight or so students living in town would be making dinner for the house that night, and we were invited to join them. The students welcomed us, in part because of their overwhelming interest in the trip we were making. Tommy and I made the most of it.

Dinner was a giant meal of spaghetti and meatballs. Our hosts encouraged us by telling us, "Eat all you want." The meal was so good that I remember it clearly. It was the first food we had eaten since the previous day, making it so enjoyable. Not only did all the uncustomary eating provide relief by quenching our hunger, but it also took eating to a new level: the feeling of a full stomach. Seemingly insignificant at the time, that feeling made the dinner even more special.

After dinner, the house evolved into a good-time party atmosphere, with many other students dropping by throughout the evening. We had fun![39] Many of our new acquaintances asked us questions about our trip. Some were curious about where we came from and what life was like in the New York City area. Others asked how we managed to get rides and what our final destination was. This interest came from genuine amazement at our trip; many were impressed by how far we had come. Many of the students were happy to help us as they discovered more about us.

As the evening wound down and darkness set in, a heavy rainstorm hit Boulder. We dreaded getting soaked while trying to hitch a ride in the dark of night. Luckily, our new friends offered to let us camp out in their living room. We were thrilled to accept their offer; it saved us from a potentially miserable night.

Our hosts welcomed us to stay as long as we wanted, so our brief stop turned into a two-day visit.

---

[39] Even though we were far too young for college, that party atmosphere was a fun place to be.

The whole Boulder escapade left us with good feelings. We had made an unexpectedly good choice in coming there and had made some real friends. As much as we liked our new friends and the town of Boulder, we decided it was time for us to get back on the road.

As we left the house with all our gear, I glanced back at the place that had been our home for the last two days with a touch of sadness. While we walked down a relatively quiet road out of town, on our way to a spot where we could hitch a ride, I spotted something lying on the road that caught my attention. I reached down to pick up a hand-rolled cigarette I knew would be a joint. I knew that marijuana was everywhere by that time but probably more prevalent in Colorado than in any other state. Finding it lying in the street gives insight into how widespread it was here in Boulder.

As Tommy and I shared the newly found smoke, we were thrilled to see a Burger King ahead. For some reason, we had the desire to devour anything. Ah, the munchies had set in, making this Burger King equivalent to hitting the jackpot.

Boulder was indeed a town with outstanding natural beauty, and the people we met there only complemented the landscape. I was disappointed that we had to leave.

ROCKY MOUNTAINS

We left Boulder and made the short trip—a couple of hours—to I-70.

I-70 runs east and west through the state of Colorado. We were psyched because I-70 would get us back on our planned route west for the first time in days. For me, the highlight of that interstate was crossing through the Rocky Mountains.

Before getting to the Rockies, we passed Golden, Colorado. Golden is home to the world's largest brewery: Coors. We had no idea what Coors was because it was a western US beer. Coors would eventually arrive in New Jersey several decades later when we could legally buy beer.

* * *

Signs announced that the Rocky Mountains, the Continental Divide, Vail, and Utah were all ahead.

As we ascended into the Rocky Mountain range, it seemed that the higher we climbed, the steeper the incline became. The ultrasteep roadway, in many places, was twisty, with numerous hairpin turns as it snaked its way up the mountain.

I was struck with the unusual sensation of gravity shifting during some of the near-vertical sections. Gravity morphed from primarily keeping my rear end on the seat to causing my back to lean firmly against the backseat. I could now look through the front windshield to see the peak and blue sky.

My ears popped multiple times as the altitude changed before we got to the summit, and assuredly did the same thing as we descended the other side.

Our ride wanted to deviate by going to Loveland Pass since it was, and probably still is, one of the most scenic mountain passes in Colorado. The friendly couple giving us a ride gave us an option: they could drop us off at the highway exit they were taking for Loveland Pass, or we could join them on their relatively short sightseeing trip. We told them we would love to see Loveland Pass if it was OK with them. They promised that after the visit, they would be returning to I-70 to continue their travels west. The side excursion was perfect since it would give us a chance to see another significant site without, most importantly, needing transportation to the site from the highway and back.

Upon reaching Loveland Pass, they parked, and we jumped out of the car to take in the spectacular views. The immediate and most impressive sight was seeing the vast mountain range, which seemed to have no end. Even in the middle of summer, the mountaintops were snow-covered.

As I stood on solid ground at the lookout point, I looked down at the clouds below us, which gave me the high feeling of being able to reach up and touch the ultraclear blue sky above.[40]

We had several views, each giving us a clear picture of our elevation. Being at the Loveland Pass pinnacle, which simultaneously was the Continental Divide, allowed us to see how far up the mountain range we had come and gave another view of how far down we had yet to go.

Wow, a long, steep way on both sides.

We could see the mountain range extending into northern Colorado and south toward New Mexico. I could see a hundred miles in both directions while standing at that site.

This kind of memorable sight is similar to looking at a picture of where you once were. Seeing the photo brings it all back as if it were today. I still have that view in my mind—no photograph needed.

Eventually, I wandered over to a National Park sign. Perhaps the Department of Interior trademarked the colors and design of the signboards.

---

[40] The moment brings to mind John Denver's tune "Rocky Mountain High." Written by John Denver and Mike Taylor and recorded in Denver in 1972, it is one of two official state songs of Colorado.

The signboard displayed two key messages: we were at Loveland Pass National Forest and were standing on the Continental Divide.[41]

Different locations along Loveland Pass, Colorado. Ski slopes and backcountry skiing area (iStock).

When our visit was finished, the four of us returned to the car and drove back to I-70. While we were traveling, the couple discussed the best way back to I-70. The discussion turned into a disagreement that resulted in the car stopping on the side of the road. The couple settled the matter after reaching an agreement based on the paper map they studied. Despite their consensus, tension remained.

Shortly after we returned to the road, they stopped at a traffic light before the entrance ramp to I-70. They both were relieved to arrive here, easing all the tension over taking the right route. They looked at each other, smiled with riveting eye contact, kissed, and proceeded to kiss again. This time, the kiss was deep, lasting longer, and their eyes were closed. Although young, I sensed the true passion of young love. If that light had only stayed red longer, I would have liked to see how that passion evolved.

---

[41] A divide separating river systems that flow to opposite sides of a continent. In North America, the line of summits of the Rocky Mountains separates streams flowing toward the Gulf of California and the Pacific from those flowing toward the Gulf of Mexico, Hudson Bay, and the Arctic Ocean.

Suddenly, horns started blasting from behind us. The driver hopped into action, realizing the light had turned green. The lasting kiss might have been interrupted; however, now all was right with the world for this young couple. Conceivably, their romance was starting to blossom.

Had they forgotten we were in the backseat? What would have happened next if there had been no traffic light? At this point, I'll leave it to our imagination.

We passed signs for many ski areas and resorts and saw a fantastic sunset as we traveled west on I-70. Colorado continued to be a beautiful state, with mile after mile of magnificent mountains; a zillion trees; and clean, fresh air.

UTAH

After leaving the Denver, Colorado, area, we traveled west on Interstate 70 toward Utah. At a certain point, we came to a sign that said, "Welcome to Utah."

I looked over at Tommy. "Hey, this is significant. It means we're only one state away from California."

With a smile and an upbeat look, he replied, "Yeah, we're finally getting there."

"I wonder where Kevin and Fast Eddie are now. Do you think they are close to California like us?"

Tommy shrugged as if to say, "I've no idea."

Neither of us realized at the time that we would need to go through part of Arizona and Nevada before arriving in California. But discovering those things added to the adventure.

After the overwhelming natural beauty of Colorado, how could Utah hold a candle to it? Utah did not disappoint. Unlike Colorado, Utah's geography was a combination of flat areas, deserts, and scattered mountains that shot straight up into the sky, many of which were snow-topped. Signs in Utah often referred to that type of steep mountain as a *peak*, different from the rolling mountains of Colorado that seemed to go on and on.

I knew from signs that we passed near several of America's most famous national parks, such as Arches and Bryce.[42] Seeing what the Rocky Mountain National Forest could offer made us want to visit, but we had

---

[42] These parks are contenders for my bucket list.

to go where the ride could take us. Hey, the rides were making this trip a reality; we stuck with them as long as they went our way.

Like viewing the new and different beautiful sights, I was also fascinated by the signs along the way. The road ones gave us direction, almost serving as a compass. Some told us roughly where we were, while others, specifically those at impressive parks, sites, or locations, often added background and history of the places we were visiting or passing by. Signs were informative throughout the entire trip.

At one point, the driver asked, "Which way are you boys going here?" I was puzzled by his question since clearly, we were going west, having traveled through most of Utah. The driver said, "You guys need to let me know your decision." I sensed impatience in his voice. Apparently, I-70 West was ending. I-70 West T-boned Interstate 15, which ran north and south.

I looked at Tommy and asked, "Which way do we go? It doesn't seem west is an option."

He glanced at me. "This is a tough one." Then he asked the driver, "Since we are headed to California, which way do you think we should go?"

Without saying a word, he answered by pointing his index finger toward the front windshield, to a large overhead sign: "North: Idaho. South: Arizona, Nevada, California." The word *California* made it an easy decision, so 15 South it was.

That segment of Utah was packed with national forests. I noted the forests and peaks because I was expecting to see the salt flats, but that didn't happen—yet. I had been unaware that mountainous terrain even existed there. After passing so many national forests, I thought that someday I would have to look up the difference between a national park and a national forest.[43]

---

[43] Perhaps the greatest difference between the two is the multiple-use mandate for national forests. While national parks are highly vested in preservation, barely altering the existing state, national forests are managed for many purposes: timber, recreation, grazing, wildlife, fish, and more.

Although still in Utah, we were close to approaching the Arizona border, when the terrain quickly changed to the desert. We were unaware that we had just entered the easternmost edge of the Mojave Desert.[44]

---

[44] Encompassing Death Valley, the hottest place in North America, the Mojave Desert is mostly in California but also spreads across southwestern Utah, southern Nevada, and northwestern Arizona. Stretching for more than forty-seven thousand square miles, including hills and basins, it also covers parts of Los Angeles and Las Vegas.

CHAPTER 26

ARIZONA, NEVADA, AND CALIFORNIA

The Welcome to Arizona sign appeared.

During the short trip through the northwest corner of Arizona, the desert seemed endless, much more so than what we had seen in Wyoming. Unlike the deep green of Colorado's hills, the Arizona hills and mountains were shades of brown, although now with a red aura cast on them from the setting sun. Colorful.

As I saw more of America, I realized I had been utterly unaware that portions of America were desert. Since I had grown up in the New York City metropolitan area, my exposure to deserts had been limited to the westerns I saw on TV and pictures in my school geography books.[45] We don't see scenes from America's deserts regularly on the evening news or anywhere in New Jersey.

Maybe I dozed off for a while, since we saw "Welcome to Nevada: The Roll-the-Dice-and-Lose-Your-Shirt State" a short time later. Well, perhaps the sign didn't say that last part, but odds are, it's safe to imply. Hey, you can always buy another shirt.

We were still on I-15, and although I didn't realize it then, the road took a bend somewhere along the way, changing from going south to now going west. Good direction!

As we traveled west through the extreme southern section of Nevada, our environment was a continuation of the same arid desert we had gone

---

[45] As a youngster, I did get some education in geography, but it probably was limited to looking at pictures with a lot of text. Around that time, I found the pictures in *National Geographic* magazine interesting.

through in Arizona. We passed numerous signs pointing out that Las Vegas was ahead. Our ride hosts—two guys who could have been our fathers—told us they were going to Vegas and gave us the option to either go into town or be let off at the exit ramp to resume our thumbing.

Since we didn't want to reveal our lack of worldly experience or appear like children, we conversed quietly. Tommy whispered, "Hey, let's check Vegas out. It sounds like a cool place."

I agreed, whispering, "We should go to one of those casinos."

Neither of us had ever been to a real casino, so we didn't know if it was true that attractive women wearing minimal clothing walked around the casino handing out free drinks. What was there to think about? We sensed that our two hosts weren't the kind of guys we could ask those types of questions.

"We could win some money in Vegas, and that's something we could use," Tommy said.

I nodded. "I guess there's a chance we could lose money too, and we can't afford that."

Disappointed, we decided Las Vegas could be a gamble and not worth the risk of losing our limited food budget, so we passed on Vegas and placed our wager on continuing with 15 West through the desert. Mature, sound reasoning and intelligent decision-making were out of character for both of us. Neither of us was comfortable that it was the correct conclusion, but as with passing gas, it was a relief to know we had made a choice.

* * *

Our next ride was from a guy in his twenties stopping for us in Nevada. He was driving a hot-spanking-new high-end sports car. It was cool looking and an example of primo comfort—one of those muscle cars with an engine that made a low gurgling sound that screamed horsepower, all while getting a good eleven miles per gallon. Considering the white-hot temperature, the air-conditioning felt good as we climbed into the ultrachic machine.

Nevada, like Arizona, was a relatively short stretch. Not long after boarding this classy car, we saw the Welcome to California sign. *What?* I was confused and surprised to see only more of the same desolate desert sand and cacti—nothing else. I'd expected to see never-ending sandy beaches with busty blonde girls tanning in skimpy bikinis, surfers riding boards on blue waves, and wood piers extending into the ocean! I didn't hear waves crashing on the sandy shore; there was no smell of ocean salt water in the air. How disappointing it was.

Well, we did have intense sunshine.

The driver of the new hot car told us he was an air force pilot. Specifically, he flew jet fighters. I thought he was probably a living magnet for girls, having this car and being a military jet pilot.

Suddenly, in the middle of nowhere, he pulled over onto the sand and informed us that he had to let us out. I asked, "Why here?" He pointed to a sign that read, "Classified High-Security US Military Base. Authorized Personnel Only. Violators Could Face Sterilization," or something to that effect. Tommy and I skipped any discussion, thanked the driver for the ride, and immediately got out of his car.

Like the scary bearded dudes in Cheyenne, Wyoming, he drove off the asphalt road onto a nondescript sand road. His cool wheels eventually disappeared, leaving the air in a whirl of dusty white sand.

"Wow," Tommy said, watching the car fade in the dust. "At least he didn't pull out a loaded gun."

"Yeah," I said as I felt the heat slam into me. "That's true, but man, it's damn hot. I can't explain why, but this looks like a much bigger desert than the one we saw in Wyoming. But what do I know?"

"I don't care what it looks like; I'm just not sure how much longer I can take it," he said with despair. I noticed that despite the high temperatures, neither of us was sweating.

I agreed, stating the obvious: "It's as hot as hell!"

That was an understatement. The sun beat down a blistering heat well over 110 degrees without a cloud in the sky. The desert looked dry. It seemed nothing could live there; it was a wild, uninhabited tract of land. Over time, I am sure that changes have occurred, but in 1970, there were zero signs of human life—I mean nothing. Fortunately, we caught another ride quickly, which was especially good since there was little traffic.

* * *

On a ride that took us a reasonable distance on I-15, we saw signs alerting motorists that I-15, which had been going west all along, would be taking a bend to the south. Signs foretold that staying on I-15 could take you to Los Angeles; Anaheim; San Diego; and Tijuana, Mexico.[46]

I had no specific idea or plan of where our most westerly California destination would be and was now beginning to realize California was a large state. Tommy and I had never discussed where we wanted to go in California. We agreed that promptly selecting a target destination might aid us. During a call home, Tommy learned that we could visit, and possibly stay at, his uncle's apartment in San Francisco. Instantly, San Francisco became our California destination.

The driver of one of our rides listened to Tommy and me try to figure out how we would get to San Francisco. He recognized that we lacked any geographic knowledge of California and did not even have a map. The driver said, "I recommend that you boys get off of I-15 ahead a short distance and take a minor but reasonably well-traveled road to one of the freeways and go north up to San Fran."

He dropped us off at the road he said would take us to the freeway. An immediate concern arose: there wasn't even an exit sign for this "reasonably well-traveled road." While it didn't cause red lights to flash, it was concerning. It seemed rather lonely. After fifteen minutes, only four or five cars passed us by—not good.

* * *

It was midsummer, and the air in the desert was molten hot. I could see the heat waves radiating off the light brown desert sand. The cacti of all shapes and sizes seemed unfazed.

We started to sense what the real problem was going to be. The bone-dry air left me feeling a thirst unlike any I had ever experienced in my lifetime. Since we had no liquids with us, the situation was becoming alarming. Gradually, my thirst concern grew into fear. I suspected that without water, we could possibly die.

It wasn't sexual companionship we were lusting for; it was water!

Our situation was now dire, to the point of being life-threatening.

---

[46] For a nanosecond, I considered obtaining a tattoo in Tijuana, showing an outline of an overweight woman wearing only a sombrero. Of course, I probably couldn't have afforded it.

Pointing down the lonely road, I said, "Hey, Tommy, do you see that house about a half mile down the road? I know it's a long walk in this heat, but maybe we can ask, beg, or do whatever it takes for some water."

Acknowledging my suggestion, he said, "Yeah, we've got to do something. Let's go."

It was fortunate that I didn't look up toward the sky. Most likely, hungry vultures were circling above us, carefully watching us, waiting for us to collapse on the desert sand. Hey, we could have been their next meal!

The dry atmosphere and the gear we were lugging, which felt extra heavy, were starting to take their toll on us physically and emotionally, arousing a feeling of doom. The penetrating rays of the sun made it unbearably hot. Despite all the physical activity (hiking and lugging our gear) in the intense heat, there was still not a single drop of sweat.

We reached the gray ranch-style house and climbed the front porch steps to ring the doorbell. The door was a darker gray than the house, with three staggered eight-by-twelve-inch glass panes. Soon a lady came to the door. She didn't open it but looked at us through one of the small windows. After fifteen seconds of looking us over, she clearly had no intention of opening the door and most likely checked to ensure the dead bolt was secure. She may have had a loaded Smith & Wesson pistol in her hand.

We started begging. I may have started screaming, "Water! Please! Water!"

With her index finger, she pointed sideways. We were confused by her persistent pointing. We looked around outside her house but saw nothing related to water. Assured there would be no verbal conversation, we gave up and left. As we were walking away from the house, I spotted an outside faucet on the side of her house! We scrambled to it as fast as we could.

Turning the knob and seeing water come out was the thrill of a lifetime. *We're going to survive!*

Tommy and I took turns sticking our open mouths underneath the water, absorbing it in massive quantities. After a while, our bellies had filled with water to the max. The feeling was outstanding. Satisfaction also came from the relief of knowing that we once again had survived a close one.

I wasn't finished. My black hair absorbed the sun's heat, making my head hot. I got down on my knees to fill up my cupped hands and started soaking my face, hair, and clothes with refreshingly cool water.

All clothes and hair were thoroughly drenched. Considering how the high temperatures affected us, the cool water gave me a sense of relief. Tommy watched me soak myself, and he proceeded to do the same.

We were as grateful for the faucet as for each ride we got that summer, but we couldn't express the "Thank you" to the woman for her water.

Amazingly, upon closing the water faucet, we picked up our gear and started down the road toward what looked like a small town. Within one minute, we were thoroughly dry, including our hair and clothes, even my underwear and socks! The rapid drying turned out to be the most amazing part of the entire incident.

We most likely didn't realize it at the time, but this was one more time when we survived what could have been a deadly event.

This incident impacted me, and it stands out as another of those lifetime memories.

CHAPTER 27

CAMPING DESERT-STYLE

Leaving the watering-hole house, we spied several buildings a half mile down the road in the direction we were traveling.

Reaching the structures, Tommy and I realized that three buildings made up the entire metropolis: a weather-beaten house that probably had seen its last coat of paint more than two decades ago, a long-abandoned single-pump gas station, and a local saloon. We reckoned we would go to the bar, not for a beer (we couldn't have afforded the beverage even if we'd wanted one; plus, there was the minor fact of our being underage) but for some more water. We were confident the ultradry air would soon make us thirsty again. This scary occasion taught us to fill up on water just in case.

We entered the saloon, passing through the two slatted swinging doors, to see an active conversation among three men sitting at the bar. The conversation came to a dead halt as they stopped to look at the pair of kids who had just walked in. I wouldn't say their faces showed shock; it was more as if they were seeing an unexpected sight. The silence continued as we approached the bar and asked the bartender for a glass of water. I am sure he was thinking, *This could be interesting.*

At least the saloon was a little cooler inside. The abundance of flies added to the establishment's ambiance.

The same array of questions Tommy and I had been asked all summer started the conversation with the three men. They were in awe, displaying a sense of disbelief that it was even possible we had hitchhiked across the country from New Jersey.

Then one asked, "Where are you sleeping tonight?"

We told them that most nights, we rolled out our sleeping bags some distance off the road.

They looked at one another, and one asked, "Have you kids ever slept in the desert before?" We hadn't.

Another one of the men said, "We know it's scorching hot out there now, but at night, things change. It gets cold—real cold. The things to be concerned about during the night are rattlesnakes. The snakes would love to join you in your warm sleeping bag until you move—then they attack, sinking their fangs into you."

I hate snakes!

"The other deadly varmints out there are scorpions. You don't want to get bit by one of them!"

Our faces probably revealed how stunned we were at that disclosure. This alarming, potentially deadly discovery was new information to us city slickers.

We'd just entered the desert zone.

As it turned out, they were nice guys, and we grew comfortable talking with them. We took their warnings as genuine advice. Undoubtedly, these local fellas had lived there for most of their lives and understood the surroundings well.

While we waited for our next ride, our discussion focused on how and where to sleep that night. Tommy said, "How about we take shifts during the night so that one of us is always up to watch out for snakes and scorpions?"

"It'll be hard without a watch, but let's take three-hour shifts. I'll take the first watch," I said.

We accepted that one of us had to be up to watch out for deadly snakes and scorpions while the other slept. We agreed on the less-than-exact three-hour shifts. It worked. We made it through the night. We were both exceedingly tired but safe from the deadly desert inhabitants. Although I never thought about it at the time, we were lucky we never really needed help, because there was no phone in the middle of the enormous Mojave Desert.[47]

---

[47] Even if we had had access to a telephone there, it wasn't until March 1973 that the White House's Office of Telecommunications issued a national policy statement that recognized the benefits of 911. By 1987, 50 percent of the US population had access to 911 emergency service numbers.

"You know, when we decided to make this trip to Califonia, I wasn't thinking about what I'd see on our journey. I sometimes thought about it on our trip here, but I neva, eva expected Califonia to be like this," I said as my extended hand swung out, pointing to the extensive desert. "In my mind, I was picturing miles of beautiful sandy beaches with people working on their suntans, surfers riding the waves on their boards, and beautiful sunshine, and I was hearing the Beach Boys' music in my background. Not this desert."

"I didn't expect it either. I hope it gets better. But, Bob, isn't it wild, all these things we're seeing as we go to different places?" Tommy responded.

"Yeah, it seems like we see new things every day. Some cool and some not so cool."

It still seemed like we weren't getting any closer to what I'd expected California to be like.

CHAPTER 28

THE FREEWAY

In New Jersey, we referred to a multilane road where trucks and cars could go balls-to-the-wall fast with no traffic lights as a *highway*. There were other descriptive labels, such as *parkway, turnpike, thruway,* and *interstate,* but regardless, all of these major arteries sometimes got constipated. The slow-going highways in California were called *freeways*.

After several more rides, we eventually made it to the 5.[48] Interstate 5 is one of California's main freeways that runs north and south through the center of the state. We chose north, in the direction of San Francisco.

* * *

When speaking with the many people we met, we always found it interesting to hear about their life experiences, especially in their area, absorbing how different it was from ours. I often found that asking people about their daily activities elicited more and sometimes enlightening personal things about them and their world. For example, if they talked about their occupation, it was often new and fascinating to us and sometimes engaging when the livelihood corresponded to the geography we were in.

The only female to give us a ride on the entire trip was an attractive Native American woman in her late twenties, along with her six-year-old son, who rode in the front seat with her. Predictively, our conversation revolved around the same questions we were asked all summer—where

---

[48] *The Five* later became a popular cable show on Fox News.

we came from, how we ate, where we slept, and so on. At one point, she cheerfully said, "Welcome to California."

I now truly felt welcomed upon reaching our destination: California.

She also shared some personal information, probably more than we needed to know or even fully understood at the time. It was interesting to hear her talk about the reservation where she'd grown up (I am choosing the word *reservation*, but it was probably more like a neighborhood of Native Americans). She went on to tell us what life was like for her now.

A major psychedelic pop hit in 1967 we knew well came on the car radio. "San Francisco (Be Sure to Wear Flowers in Your Hair)" was timely, arousing a special feeling of being in the moment and our current destination.

Wow, here we are right now, approaching San Francisco. We felt a strong need to put flowers in our hair. I asked our driving host, "Would you mind pulling to the side so we can pick some flowers for our hair?"

She found our request humorous, so with a big smile, she said, "Fine," and she pulled the Ford Country Squire station wagon with faux wood side panels over to the side of the freeway.[49]

I had no idea if there might be flowers on the side of the freeway. We didn't even give it thought, but there were plentiful varieties of colorful flowers. Tommy and I quickly picked a bunch of them and returned to the car. The driver found our impromptu hairstyling for arriving in San Francisco hysterically funny.

She assured us the flowers were appropriate for San Francisco. We proceeded to put the freshly picked flowers into our hair while her son continued to stare at the two peculiar strangers. Eventually, we got off the 5, catching a ride that took us into an impoverished section of the City by the Bay. As we walked the streets of San Francisco, we still had most of the flowers in our hair, so I thought we blended in nicely.

* * *

Tommy and I had been hungry for hours by that point. It had been close to forty-eight hours since we last had eaten anything. We agreed that getting something to eat again took precedence over everything.

---

[49] The station wagon was *the* family vehicle prior to the SUV.

As we walked along the city sidewalk, we looked in the windows of eateries. We doubted there would be a McDonald's or Burger King in that area. We immediately ruled out places with a maître d' and genuine tablecloths (not that there were many in that part of town). It took us only ten seconds to realize that the dining places we passed were beyond our sparse finances, so we kept moving. We were growing hungrier and becoming frustrated.

I asked a boy in the street—approximately eleven or twelve years old—if he knew of a place to get some food and told him we didn't have much money. He pointed a block away and said, "The fish place." Tommy and I found the fish place and learned they only had one item on the menu: fish and chips.

We agreed to splurge, spending three dollars (somewhat above budget) to order one meal to share.

It was no mystery why this hole-in-the-wall dining extravaganza was inexpensive. The square footage was no larger than a good-sized closet. When empty, assuming all were standing, the order and waiting area could only support four people, six if they were squeezed sardine-style. Stacking all our gear didn't help with the limited space and eliminated room for two people.

The only light coming in the place was through the street window; plus, it had a red neon *Fish* light in the front window. The light's tubing had numerous blacked-out blotches, whether from age, lack of maintenance, or grease splatter (likely all combined), that affected its poor condition.

In the back, above the fryer, a new yellow box of Preparation H sat on an old, dirty metal shelf.

The radio in the background played some unidentifiable foreign music. The linoleum-tiled floor contained petrified dirt, grease, and grime. The inside of the takeout joint had the aroma of a latrine last serviced four years ago.

We were so hungry that we didn't care. We needed *something* to eat!

Our fish-and-chips order was almost ready after a few minutes, not much longer than Mickey D's. I assumed the one man we saw wore many hats, such as chef (maybe a stretch), waiter, concierge, cashier, finance manager, and owner. He assuredly didn't have hygiene hang-ups.

My impression was that he was grossly unconcerned about how others viewed his appearance, as evidenced by his unkempt, greasy hair; four days of beard growth; small yet colorful facial tattoos; and nose ring, my first actual nose ring sighting. The tarnished ring appeared, quite possibly, to be genuine gold.

It made me wonder, *How does one go about polishing a nose ring? How does he blow his nose? Maybe he doesn't. Ouch—how painful was it getting that thing installed? Although I would never ask, was it worth it?*

All my prior familiarity with nose rings was from watching pirate cartoons on my family's black-and-white TV, usually with my brothers at ridiculously early times on Saturday mornings.

Based on his appearance, he did not appear to be the kind of wholesome man you would like your daughter to bring home to meet Mom and Dad, albeit he did fit right in with the neighborhood we were currently in, so maybe I shouldn't have been so quick to judge.

The preparation of our order (nothing to do with the yellow box) was almost complete. Mr. Clean pulled out two or three newspaper pages and spread them on the small counter. The man then pulled out a basket from the fryer and emptied different-looking, huge french fries (later, I would learn to call them *steak fries*) onto the newspaper and then turned around and emptied a separate basket of four huge pieces of breaded fish. He wrapped up our food in the newspaper and collected our cash, and after grabbing our gear, we quickly squeezed our way out onto the sidewalk with our bounty.

Sadly, I suddenly realized the flowers were no longer in my hair.

I didn't know it then, but I would later learn this type of fish is the secret to the popular fish-and-chips dish. Any fish other than Pacific cod makes it an impostor.

San Francisco is famous for its cable cars, the Golden Gate Bridge, the former Alcatraz Federal Penitentiary,[50] and fish and chips. Other items the city is known for I've intentionally left out.

We stood out on the sidewalk, holding the bundle of food wrapped in newspaper. It was still daylight, and the roads were becoming busy with cars, trucks, and taxis weaving their way through rush-hour traffic. The

---

[50] The prison closed in 1963, and the island is now a major tourist attraction managed by the National Park Service.

sidewalk was packed with people navigating their way home or to a nearby shelter. We stood there wondering, *Where do we eat our meal?*

We were in a not-so-great section in the middle of a city. There were no parks or benches we could sit on.

Hunger was overruling all else. There were no options other than to sit down on the sidewalk. Enjoying the comfort of the hard sidewalk, we relaxed by leaning back against a building wall, separated by a drainpipe. We dropped the newspaper package onto the cement between us. We proceeded to enjoy our meal amid the petrified gum blotches, small pieces of shattered wine bottles, blood, spit, and vomit residue, which was now our tablecloth.

People walking the sidewalk didn't glance at us, and to avoid getting trampled on or tripping walkers, we sat cross-legged.

While it could have been primarily due to extreme hunger, it was one of the best meals I enjoyed over the two-and-a-half-month trip. Another factor was that my palate wasn't exactly what I would call refined at sixteen.

We ate until we could no longer take another bite. Despite our initial concern that the food might be insufficient, surprisingly, it turned out to be twice what we could consume. We wrapped up the remaining fish and potatoes in the newspaper and offered them to a young man who looked in need of a meal. His eyes lit up at the offer, and he thanked us several times as he walked off with the newspaper-wrapped survival package.

I figure that over the last fifty years, I have probably eaten 54,871 meals. I find it amazing that this one particular dinner stands out so clearly.

We forgot to say grace.

* * *

"Hey, Tommy, are you up to seeing if Haight-Ashbury is around here?"

His eyes opened wider, and he nodded. "Absolutely. Let's ask someone how close it is. My uncle isn't expecting us anytime soon, so let's do it."

We learned that it was within walking distance, and we had just eaten a full meal and felt good, so we took off for our next destination: Haight-Ashbury.

Haight-Ashbury is a district in the central part of San Francisco. It is the West Coast version of the East Village on the lower east side of

Manhattan, New York City. Both coastal city sections attracted hippies, drug culture, peace, love, and a new kind of political thought, including flower power, in the late 1960s and early '70s.

Up-and-coming rock bands knew they made the big time if invited to perform at either the Fillmore West in San Francisco or the Fillmore East in New York. The best rock bands from the United States and Britain played at these two venues, making numerous live recordings while performing there.[51]

Since we were in San Francisco, this was our chance to investigate the Haight-Ashbury neighborhood. We ended up in the Golden Gate Park area known as Hippie Hill. The area became renowned because it captivated the counterculture movement, especially the hippie subculture culminating in Haight Street's 1967 Summer of Love event overflowing right onto what is now called Hippie Hill. In the three years since 1967, I doubt it changed, and I guess the area is still locked into that '60s era even today.

Most of the people there were older than we were, but they all seemed to be members of the hippie cult crowd. Here would have been the ideal place to have the flowers in our hair.

In a park in the Haight-Ashbury neighborhood, a man approached us and said, "You guys want to buy some acid?"

The stranger's unexpected question caused Tommy and I to give each other a "Sure, why not?" look. Still somewhat unsure, I asked, "How much?"

He answered, "Buck a tab."

Without any discussion, we made the purchase. After swallowing our tab (pill), we began our first LSD trip.

The trip was a psychedelic experience causing us to laugh at visual hallucinations, which I saw with my eyes open or closed—meaningless, colorful, kaleidoscopic cartoons. Other senses impacted us less, including

---

[51] On a personal note, I attended my first big-time rock concert at the Fillmore East on May 17, 1969. My ticket cost $3.75 to see Chuck Berry, B. B. King, and the Who. The Who performed the rock opera *Tommy*; it was the same day the studio album *Tommy* was released in the United States. At the concert, I had my first experience smoking marijuana, or pot, weed, herb, or whatever you want to call it.

taste, and we had expanded, vivid imaginations. We laughed so hard at times that tears rolled down our cheeks.

At no point were we impaired.

I need to make an important point here. I have shared this particular event because it was part of what happened on this summer trip. In no way am I suggesting that anyone try LSD, as I later knew others who had severe adverse reactions, not to mention the legal implications. Enough said.

We still minimally felt the effects when we arrived at Tommy's uncle's large apartment. His uncle was a nice guy, and so were his three roommates, who greeted us, showing interest in our trip. They let us roll out our sleeping bags on their living room floor, where we slept comfortably, this time without fear of rattlesnakes and scorpions.

We woke up the following morning and realized the men were gone, probably off to work.

"I saw a clock in the other room. We definitely slept later today than we usually do," I said to Tommy.

"Yeah, probably because there wasn't a rising sun to wake us," he said.

Taking advantage of having the apartment to ourselves, we relaxed, enjoying the rare luxury of some TV. After a few hours, we packed our gear and lazily launched into another new day of our adventure.

That day would be different.

CHAPTER 29

THE PARTY-RIDE ESCAPE

Interstate 80 runs east and west more than three thousand miles across America, contiguous between New York and San Francisco.[52] After more than a month and more than four thousand miles of traveling west, that day marked the first time we would navigate another three thousand miles going east—to the place we called home. After more than six weeks of traveling west, going east just seemed wrong.

We got an unusually late start. We commenced the day by catching our first ride through the city to where I-80 began going east, but our second ride that morning was truly memorable.

A car slowed, pulled over, and stopped on the freeway shoulder. It was a polished, shiny red convertible with the top down, making the most of the warm, sunny California day. At the wheel was a man in his thirties, and four girls in their twenties rode with him. All of them cheered us to join them—this was different.

We ran (it was bad form to keep a potential ride waiting) to the car, hauling along all our gear. Getting into the car wasn't going to be easy, considering the limited seating space, the floor littered with empty beer cans, a new case of Boone's Farm Apple Wine (I assumed to be twelve

---

[52] Interstate 80 (I-80) is an east–west transcontinental freeway that crosses the United States from downtown San Francisco, California, to Teaneck, New Jersey, in the New York City metropolitan area. The highway was designated in 1956 as one of the original routes of the Interstate Highway System; its final segment was opened in 1986.

bottles), and three stacked cases of beer. Eventually, we did squeeze in—a tight fit—with the girls. No complaints.

The driver apparently had consumed at least one case of beer by himself already, and the four girls decided to help out. How considerate of them.

He shot his hot car onto the freeway, burning rubber and swerving between lanes at sound-barrier-breaking speed. The driver didn't seem to have any noticeable anxiety about the police or anything else as we breezed through Sacramento, the capital of California.

The wild ride was scary for me when he twice made hard close-call turns while shifting between cars and jumping lanes, all in a matter of seconds. I considered it vital to hold on to something stable to prevent myself from being ejected due to a sudden, and highly likely, veer. It would have been an ideal time for a seat belt; however, there were none.

With the traffic noise, the blasting radio, and the loud wind caused by the convertible's speed, I had to raise my voice to say, "Tommy, we need to be careful. The way this guy cuts between lanes—hold on to something—hey, we could get thrown out of the car!"

"Yeah, I am holding on, and I'm not worried. This is a fun ride. So the beer isn't cold—it still works."

The other drivers on the freeway frequently honked their horns and used expressive hand gestures as Mr. I. M. Smashed weaved among the traffic.

"Hey, this guy is for sure bombed," Tommy said.

"Yeah, I noticed. At least the congested traffic is easing up."

Compared to how it is enforced fifty years later, in 1970, driving under the influence (DUI) often was not necessarily as major a legal infraction unless there were specific circumstances. Depending on where you were and who you knew, it's possible to even get off with a warning. It was illegal, and you could end up getting a ticket for it as long as there was no accident, injury, or death.

Frequent stops on the side of the road added public urination to the day's shopping list of prosecutable activities. The four girls made this a group project by running out of sight behind bushes. I assume they used the "drip-dry" method. *Oh, if I'm caught, my mother would be so disappointed.*

Mr. I. M. Smashed encouraged us to drink as much as possible. He confidently announced, "If we run out, we'll stop to get more. Let's get this shindig in gear!" He told us not to be bashful. "The beverage supply is guaranteed." Everything was under control.

"Hey, Bob, free beer—this is pretty good," Tommy said with a smile. "Almost too good to be true."

The party on wheels got loud at times. The party atmosphere included yelling, laughing, music blasting from the car radio or 8-track tape player, loud and auxiliary sounds of amplified car horns, and truck traffic. Only noisemakers were missing. The floating celebration moved on; the beverages continued to flow.

Eventually, the girls alerted Mr. Smashed that their stop was approaching. The girls stumbled out; the automobile rolled on.

The Sacramento radio station was starting to crackle and fade, so I. M. turned off the radio, giving me an unexpected feeling of relief from the interviews, talk, pop music, and endless commercials. The reduced noise instilled a sense of calm.

The traffic eased more the farther east we traveled.

Either the liquor was finished (at least the beer), or the thirsts had been quenched. The atmosphere became quieter. The calm allowed us to have a conversation for the first time now that the spirits were starting to wear off.

In this new serenity, I. M. Smashed opened up and shared that he had escaped from an institution that treated behavioral disorders, the type often associated with alcohol abuse. After he broke out, he stole this nice red convertible, bought a good supply of sauce, and was now bolting for the state line.

The more I. M. told us, the more aware we became that just by being in the car, we could face consequences also if the police caught up with him.

"Do you think if the cops catch us, we'll end up in jail?" I asked Tommy.

"Nah, we didn't do anything wrong, and they're probably looking for him for doing more than stealing this car."

I had to agree with him. It was a little scary at times, but so far, so good; plus, this was a fun ride covering a good distance.

Undoubtedly, at least in my mind, California law enforcement had had a BOLO out for him for hours, including the boosted car we were in. It also explained the many signs indicating Reno, Nevada, was ahead.

We were getting out of California, which was OK with us as long as he was going east.

We crossed the state line into Nevada; I. M. heaved a sigh of relief.

It was getting dark as we entered Reno. In my mind, I assumed Reno was a miniature, low-class version of Las Vegas, including all the casinos, hotels, cheap motels, and bright neon lights.

Upon entering Reno, I saw a massive multicolored neon sign depicting a roping cowboy on a bucking horse—a real attention-getter.

I didn't consider Reno a location that attracted the big whales, compared to those who usually arrived in Vegas on their private jets and plopped down $100,000 bets. Reno struck me as a down-on-your-luck kind of town where most gamblers placed their big bets on the penny and nickel slot machines.

I. M. Smashed was starting to fade as the day of heavy drinking took its toll. He visibly struggled to keep his eyes open and announced he needed to stop there to get some sleep. "I'll get you guys a hotel room for the night if you want."

Without hesitation, we accepted I. M.'s offer. Less than a minute later, he pulled the shiny red convertible into a budget-minded motel parking lot long overdue for repair and said, "You guys wait in the car." After checking us in, he came out, handed us our room key, and told us to pack up our gear since he was going to "a different place." I wondered who he'd checked us in as—Bob and Tommy? After thanking him for the ride and his generosity of the hotel room, he disappeared somewhere deep into the bowels of Reno. Maybe he was looking for a place to vomit or ditch the car.

* * *

The two-bed motel room included a bathroom; a chance to shower, including much-needed soap, more flower-garden-scented shampoo, and clean towels; and the added bonus of TV.

The comfortable mattress was a bit worn but a welcome relief compared to sleeping on the hard floor at Tommy's uncle's apartment. Perhaps most important was the pleasure of a real pillow.[53]

---

[53] On this trip, I started to develop an affection for a pillow with a clean pillowcase. I guess it's one of those things that's easy to take for granted if it's always been there waiting for you every night.

I felt refreshed as I lay wallowing in a real bed with clean sheets. The bedsheets were tremendous since it was the only night we'd slept in a bed with sheets, or an actual pillow, on the entire trip. The impact of sheets was more significant since our sleeping bags were starting to get a little grungy.

"Wow, what a ride today—and a long ride at that!" Tommy said with a content smile.

"Yeah, a roller coaster of one, like a party on wheels with the booze, in a fast stolen car. It got wild at times."

"It was cool of him to buy us this motel room."

"Yeah, that was cool. I feel sorry for him some. I think he has a long road in front of him and hope he can deal with his issues; it sounds like he has a bunch," I said.

The following day, we packed up and hitched rides to get us back on I-80 East.

"Hey, Tommy, we made it to California! Is that cool or what?" I said with an accomplished smile.

"Yeah, it's really something, but now we gotta get all the way back," he said, agreeing about our success.

On our first ride that day, we heard on the radio about some type of planned legalization of prostitution. Neither of us felt comfortable asking the stranger giving us the ride, "What's all this about legal prostitution?" so we kept quiet.

But Tommy looked at me with somewhat raised eyebrows, as if to say, *What's this all about?*

I returned the facial expression. *Hell if I know.*

We kept hearing the breaking news on car radios that a Nevada county was now in the process of passing its first ordinance to license brothels.[54]

Several rides later, I finally said to the driver, "We keep hearing about this legalized prostitution. What do you think about it?"

"Lately, everyone is calling the county the new law impacts the Erogenous Zone. Well, there's really nothing new about it. These places have been around these here parts for as long as I've been. The ones they're talking about on the radio, like the well-known Mustang Ranch in the

---

[54] Since the mid-1800s, prostitution has flourished in western areas, such as California, Arizona, Colorado, and other regions of the new territory. Only Nevada allows legal prostitution in the United States.

Reno area, are tourist traps. Most all that business frankly takes place at millions of smaller illegal places."

I know what you are thinking, and no, we didn't.

Without incident, we continued to travel east on I-80, heading toward Utah.

CHAPTER 30

UTAH REVISITED

Utah was one of the states we went through twice. We'd traveled through southern Utah on our way west to California; we were now going through the northern section of Utah as we headed east. Comparing northern to southern Utah was interesting, especially seeing the considerable geographic differences within the state.[55]

We were unaware that we left Pacific time and entered mountain daylight time when crossing the line from Nevada into Utah.[56]

For some reason, entering Utah made me think, *Wow, we're really headed home.* Even though our expedition was now focused eastward, I still felt the same excitement I'd felt when we started the trip in June. I knew there was no way we could know or anticipate what might happen during this segment of our journey; all along, I remained confident that multiple unforeseen episodes were yet to happen.

We couldn't miss the signs for the salt flats region, otherwise known as the Great Salt Lake Desert.

Driving on the salt flats was permissible, but signs reminded you that doing so was at your own risk. Our ride had neither time nor interest in taking his car for a spin on the salt flats. *I mean, really, how risky could it be?* I thought.

---

[55] States we went through twice other than Utah included Nevada, Wyoming, Illinois, Indiana, and Ohio.

[56] Hawaii and Arizona are the only US states, with the exception of the Navajo Nation, that do not utilize daylight saving time.

We drove past the Great Salt Lake, a considerable body of water, about fifty miles after passing the salt flats.

Another fifty miles beyond the lake, we took an exit off I-80 and pulled into Salt Lake City.

My only real experience with cities in my first sixteen years was New York City, though I now had had a taste of Denver and San Francisco. Salt Lake City opened my eyes to something different. It was a far newer city, and what stood out to me most was how *clean* it was. It seemed free of garbage, litter, and spray-painted graffiti, and even the trash cans were clean!

Our brief stop in Salt Lake City allowed us to insert coins into a vending machine for our daily meal, and then our driver steered the car back onto I-80 East again.

* * *

Utah borders two states to its east. Wyoming lies northeast of Utah, while Colorado adjoins central and southeastern Utah. Traveling east on I-80 took us into Wyoming. I-80 ran west and east along southern Wyoming, not far from the Colorado line.

We picked up our next and final ride in Utah east of Salt Lake City as we approached the Wyoming state line. A nondescript black panel van without any markings stopped for us—an indistinct type of vehicle we often hear reported on the evening news. For example, "Sure, Sean, Police Chief Dick Otens tells me an eyewitness saw three or four perpetrators quickly leaving the jewelry store just behind me in a panel van. The witness is sure the van's color was either black, dark brown, or possibly tan; unfortunately, he could not identify a license plate or provide police with a make or model or estimate the age of the van. Reporting, Brian Roberts, KBS 6 News."

The van's back doors opened; we loaded our gear and climbed in. Each of the two rear doors contained a small window that let in some light, less since sundown was moments away. The only other window was the windshield. Since we were in the back of the van, it was dark, with nothing to see.

In the van were four men in their late twenties and early thirties.

The van floor was ridged of hard metal—very uncomfortable. We eventually rolled out our sleeping bags to provide our derrieres added comfort. Any comfort faded fast.

It felt like we were in a dark cave without any light. This good long ride covering much ground was starting to be a drag.

A gasoline smell was consistent. Though not especially strong, it never seemed to go away. It was nothing anyone seemed concerned about.

While Tommy and I chatted, there was more conversation among the four men; they seemed to have no interest in us, not even the typical questions and conversation we were accustomed to. But what we heard them talk about got our attention. There were occasional discussions recollecting some of their past exploits.

"Hey, you guys remember doing that liquor store job in Texas?" one of the guys in the back said to the three toward the front. "That kid behind the counter was scared shitless when we pulled out the guns." All four got a good laugh at the recollection.

The passenger added, "We got double lucky that night. We never expected a liquor store would have that much cash, and that was one razor-close call with the fuzz arriving as fast as they did. We were super lucky we didn't get busted that night."

Tommy and I were quiet as we concentrated on listening to their conversation. We didn't talk, since we didn't want them to hear any of our comments on what we thought about their burglary.

Later, they talked about occasions when they'd heisted cars. After boosting a car, they would take it to an underground auto shop that typically would tear the car apart and sell the parts on the black market.

The sociopath kleptos took turns driving, with one of them usually sleeping. The guy who had been in the back reminiscing about the liquor store holdup was now driving, Raising his voice so the other three could hear him, he said, "Remember the eighteen-wheeler job?"

The passenger-seat guy said, "Yeah, we made some cake on that one. Too bad Jimmy ain't around no more to give us scoops on jobs like that one since he got pinched in New York. I think he's doing a nickel in Sing Sing."

"Jimmy's cut on those jobs was always fair," one of the guys now in the back said.

The quietest of the four in the back said, "That's the one Lou rented—the box truck we used to load the TVs and other shit from the trailer.

The best part was when we finished—driving the truck into the lake and watching it sink." The four of them laughed at the memory.

I now believed our ride was with four career criminals. We never knew if past rides were from criminals, but with this ride, well, there was no question.

Taking a quick look at Tommy, I saw he was leaning back against the van siding, staring off into space. To get his attention, I tapped his foot. He turned to look at me. I could see the fear on his deadpan face and realized it was precisely how I felt.

Just when I thought I was beginning to understand who the guys were, they would say something that further defined who they were. Nothing about it was good.

"Hey, Mike, do you still have those AR-15s?" the passenger asked the driver.[57]

"Sure, I got 'em, but not much ammo left after doin' dat boat."

Their conversation was sketchy at times, but I realized they were talking about a drunken night when they had come across a yacht tied up at a dock, presumably at a lake. Using Mike's AR-15s, for fun, they'd pumped a couple hundred rounds into the boat's hull. Since their objective had been to sink the yacht completely, they had been disappointed that it only fell over onto its side. At least they were consoled in knowing that whoever owned it would never use it again.

Really? This is what these guys do for fun?

We were absorbing everything these bad guys were saying. The more conversation we heard, the more we became alarmed. What about the times when they whispered about something so we wouldn't listen? Indeed, it was better that we didn't hear those stories.

We reached a point where the lack of any conversation was starting to make it uncomfortable for our hosts (if you could call them that) and us. We weren't laughing with them about their lawless escapades; there was no meaningful discussion.

Who are these guys, and how concerned should we be?

---

[57] While there are variations of the AR-15 (commonly referred to as an assault rifle), it essentially is a .223-caliber gas-operated semiautomatic rifle that is essentially a civilian version of the M16. The gun magazine typically holds twenty rounds.

The van continued to roll on through the night. The ride could easily have qualified as a red-eye.

It was probably around midnight and very dark inside and outside the van when we drifted into an unrestful sleep. It was a painful doze, as the metal floor gave birth to pains in areas of the body that had never hurt before. Over time, each tiny bounce or vibration the van made felt like being hit by a sledgehammer.[58]

After approximately five hours, we moved quickly through the length of Wyoming without seeing anything. It was disappointing since we had seen so much beauty there on the way west.

* * *

Somewhere between three and four in the morning, the van took an exit. It was enough of a reduced speed, sound, and feeling of the centrifugal force generated by the tight turn of the ramp for the combined sensations to pull us out of our shut-eye, arousing awareness that something was changing.

Undoubtedly, we had covered a lot of ground while traveling nonstop for almost eight hours.

The van drove off the exit into a quiet residential area of modest homes. We were now in residential Middle America, the breadbasket of the United States, and the setting of *The Greatest Generation*.[59] The neighborhood had well-kept houses, lit streetlights, and organized yards, each with a well-kept lawn. I imagined each house as a home filled with hardworking families all getting their night's sleep, including the dog.

When the van initially stopped to give us a ride, we climbed in and were hit by the unmistakable smell of gasoline. We learned that the van was carrying five military-grade five-gallon steel gas cans, the kind mounted on the back of army jeeps.

A congregation of male crickets trying to generate enough noise to win a mate's heart was the only sound I heard.

After we parked, everyone got out of the van. The crooks focused on

---

[58] How is it the memory of a single night's sleep, or something close to sleep, can be remembered so clearly so many years later?

[59] A compelling book written by Tom Brokaw about how the working nation banded together to support our military fighting in World War II.

us, explaining that they got all their gas by pulling into towns like this in the middle of the night to siphon it from parked cars. Like passing gas, they did it every day.

"We'll give you guys a can to fill. Do it quickly and quietly," one of the gang members said.

I innocently told the ethics-deprived livery drivers, "I don't think stealing is right."

Clearly, that didn't go over well. Mike, the owner of the assault rifles, took a step closer and stared me in the eye. Keeping his voice low to avoid attracting attention, he said threateningly, "Listen, you assholes. You've got a choice. Either go fill up a can, or start walking." Mike's face displayed a combination of anger and a total loss of patience. Lack of sleep probably played a role as well.

Tommy was unusually quiet—he was never quiet—throughout the intensifying tension. I quickly recalled their discussion about using guns in robberies and the sailboat incident. I didn't hesitate to provide a somewhat defiant response: "We'll fill the fuckin' can." It was slightly out of character for me.

This depraved guy has the audacity to call us assholes?

We likely avoided a violent standoff, and they supplied us with one empty five-gallon can and a narrow, flexible twenty-inch-long black rubber tube. We were as quiet as possible to avoid attention as we got ten seconds of whispered instructions. They told us how to siphon using the rubber tube, which meant sticking one end into the car's gas tank and the other end in our mouths and then sucking it like a straw.[60] Once we got a mouthful of gas, we had to quickly pull the tube out of our mouths and stick it in the gas can, causing the flow of gasoline from the car tank into the gas can. If you have never had a mouthful of gasoline, take my word for it: it's nothing like pink lemonade.

Since there were plenty of cars parked in driveways, I quietly told Tommy, "Rather than completely draining the tank of this car, let's stop at a point and continue to fill up using another car. This way, when they get up in the morning, they'll at least be able to use the car."

"Yeah, OK."

---

[60] It was similar to sucking on a straw to drink a glass of soda, but instead of soda, it was gasoline, and we really tried to avoid drinking it.

It took siphoning from several cars to fill our can; then we had to get the can back to the van.

"Shit, this can is brutally heavy now that it's full," I quietly gasped to Tommy.

"Let's take turns."

I readily agreed to his plan, but that didn't make moving it any easier; the full five-gallon can of gasoline was very heavy for two skinny, somewhat malnourished boys, forcing us to take turns carrying it. Eventually, we made it back to the van to complete the despicable task.

The low-life thieves, true derelicts of society, negligent of understanding any difference between right and wrong, had indeed developed expertise in swiftly completing a process in the stillness of the night. They had already filled the van's gas tank (I had no idea how many trips it had taken to acquire the gas) and then filled and packed four gas cans into the back of the van. They gave us looks of tired impatience as we struggled to get our single can up and into the van.

The tension I sensed was becoming uncomfortable for everyone. The four guys were indeed dissatisfied with how long it had taken us to do our end of the gasoline rip-off.

After replenishing the gas stockpile, we rapidly jumped into the van and made a clean getaway back onto I-80 East.

I didn't feel guilty about the gas rip-off. I considered it a matter of survival. Who knew what those guys might have done to us if we hadn't cooperated? Did they have guns in the van now? What other scenarios would they try to have us involved with? I presumed the stories we'd heard in the van from the depraved guys were true. What spooked me the most were the unknowns that could be ahead of us.

For the entire trip, almost all rides came from nice people who were friendly and kind enough to help us with our journey. Those guys were the opposite. *I guess it takes all kinds.*

Only a few minutes back on I-80, I leaned over close to Tommy's ear and whispered, "These guys are nuts, and I'm gettin' scared they might do something to us."

"Yeah, let's get off this wagon train."

"OK, I'll tell 'em we need to get off at the next exit."

Tommy and I quietly decided it was time to disconnect from these guys.

I said, "Hey, we need to get off at the next exit," speaking loudly enough for the band of thieves to hear me. They acknowledged my request, presumably glad to get rid of us—a simple failure to bond.

There were only two times on the entire trip when we chose not to stay with someone going our way for the entire ride—this was one of them. The other was the desperate need for food when we couldn't wait any longer.

The panel van dropped us off somewhere in western Nebraska as the sun rose. There was a feeling of relief in getting out of that van and away from the crooks. Since the sun was now up, it was great to see the world around, compared to the coffin-like darkness inside the van.

We were still on I-80, the same highway we had taken when leaving New Jersey on day one, the same freeway leaving San Francisco. In 1970, I-80 in the Midwest was a simple two-lane road that ran through endless cornfields. This was a significant difference compared to the high-speed multilane thoroughfares of I-80 at either end of the country.

It was late morning, and we had covered some ground via multiple shorter rides going through the extended state of Nebraska. Next to no sleep the night before resulted in exhaustion, and it began to take its toll.

CHAPTER 31

AWAKENING

We cheered up when a black sedan pulled over to give us a ride. I placed the car somewhere between the 1958 and 1961 model years.

Driving was a prematurely balding man, most likely in his early fifties. He was with his wife, whom I estimated to be in her late forties, and their son, who we later learned was seven. All three sat in the front seat of the older, roomy car.

Tommy and I clambered into the spotless and spacious rear seat. Cars were built like tanks in the late 1950s and typically included sizable gas-guzzling engines. They had convenient features like cigarette lighters and built-in ashtrays for smokers, all considered basic requirements by auto manufacturers during that time. Some manufacturers started to offer seat belts as an option in the early 1960s. However, seat belts were not mandatory in the United States until 1966.

Auto air-conditioning had become so popular that by 1969, more than half of all new cars sold were equipped with AC.

Early auto air-conditioning became available as an add-on.

For the umpteenth time, we answered the same questions about where we came from; where we were going; how we ate, drank, and slept; and other pertinent details essential for human survival.

The question-and-answer period always contained our mainly selfish question to the driver: "Where are you going?" We wanted to calculate how far the ride would take us.

On this car ride, the conversation flowed, as this family were cordial and genuinely seemed happy to meet us and to help us on our adventure by simply giving us a ride.

The driving father was excited to tell us they had just purchased the car. He said, "This is my first new car, and you're the first people we are giving a ride." He spoke with a beaming smile on his face. It was the kind of smile that screamed pride. Since the car was not showroom new, I assumed he was saying, "This is my first car."

The first thing we noticed about the mom was that she had several large white bandages on her face and a substantial area of her head. The bandages appeared amateurish, possibly homemade, certainly not something a hospital emergency room or doctor's office would have applied. When we asked, "What happened?" the pause in conversation spoke that we unknowingly had hit a tender subject they weren't prepared to discuss.

The father finally responded, "My wife has epilepsy," and left it at that.

I knew epilepsy was a neurological condition resulting in various types of seizures. The seizures, also known as convulsions, often cause the individual to lose consciousness, sometimes leading to a fall. Hence, seizures often result in injuries similar to the mother's. I was all too aware of epilepsy.

The seven-year-old boy spent the entire half hour turned around, facing backward, with his eyes riveted on Tommy and me.

As we got close to their home, the mother asked, "Would you boys like to have lunch with us?"

Since we never turned down a free meal, we gratefully replied, "Yes."

We had no way of knowing the impact accepting this invitation would ultimately have on us.

* * *

As we were approaching their home, the north side of I-80 seemed like miles of cornfields. Each row of corn appeared uniformly neat and organized.

The south side of the road was open, flat land where I saw the wind blowing tumbleweeds and some stationary low-level bushes. One could easily see this wasteland for a mile in either direction since there were no trees or hills.

We made a right-hand turn off I-80 onto a dirt road. Within a hundred yards were five homes. Each appeared identical in every way.

The outside of the house had the standard four sides, some small windows, and a roof. Each house contained one floor, with cinder blocks supporting and elevating the wood-framed home a couple of feet off the ground. The same cinder blocks also acted as the front porch steps leading to the door.

Each house had a shingled roof, adding a touch of extravagance to the home.

Notably, the exterior of each house consisted of planks of unprotected raw wood slightly thicker than plywood. Evidencing years of exposure, the weather-beaten wood was now a dark brown and warped in places. Gaps stood out since you could see between the planks in many areas.

Even with no carpentry experience, I could see that the construction of the homes was sloppy and haphazard at best.

I doubted there was heat, although there appeared to be no shortage of ventilation. *How could anyone survive the cold in the winter?*

That type of home construction must have generated excitement during threats of hurricanes and tornadoes. Tornadoes were not something we dealt with in the New York City area, but I got the impression they frequently occurred in that part of the country.

The community landscaping mainly was dirt, with occasional weeds and scattered wild, unkempt bushes, certainly not provided by a landscaper.

When the driver parked the car, they invited us into their home. We took the cinder-block steps into the predominantly unfurnished, empty house. As I walked into the house, it immediately hit me that the floorboards were not lined up against one another, giving clear sight of the ground below the house.

They invited us to have a seat. There were five mismatched chairs, so we sat down at their single table and talked while the mother prepared lunch in the kitchen. I guessed they had running water, probably a propane-powered stove, and maybe a refrigerator, although I never saw one.

Under more normal circumstances, I would have politely asked to use the bathroom; however, I didn't want to deal with "We don't have one," which I anticipated might be the likely response.

I got a quick partial glimpse of the kitchen and saw the mother stirring something in a pot on the stove. I noted that the countertop consisted of more wooden boards supporting a cardboard box labeled Lipton Instant Cup-a-Soup. We knew lunch was about to be served when the mother set five spoons on the table. Like the chairs, no two spoons appeared to have been made by the same manufacturer. The mother served hot soup for lunch, bringing in one plate at a time. She apologized for not having enough bowls as she served us.

On the table were two small bowls from the same set and one unique plate with raised edges, working as a small soup bowl. Since there were no more dishes, our soup came in an upside-down pot lid. We used one hand to keep the top steady to prevent it from spilling since it could not lie flat.

When we finished lunch, we said our goodbyes along with a sincere thank-you to them for giving us the ride, inviting us into their home, and feeding us a fabulous lunch. Most importantly, we expressed our genuine appreciation for their generosity.

As Tommy and I started the short walk up the dirt road to I-80, I said, "Tommy, I don't think I've ever seen poverty quite like that before."

"Me neither. My doghouse is built better than their house. I wonder how they survive in the winter."

"Here, all along, I've been thinking we're eating lean."

For sure, this family lacked sufficient food, medical care, and basic shelter. Sure, many people have a tough time making ends meet, but seeing how this family lived had a major impact on me. Possibly, some of it was because I was only sixteen at the time. Regardless, it gave me a dose of reality and certainly humbled me for a lifetime. It may have been the first time I fully recognized how blessed I was. It gave me a feeling of gratefulness for my fortunate life.

Of the more than three hundred rides we had that summer, this one was truly unforgettable. For the rest of my life since then, the mention of chicken noodle soup has triggered the emotional memory originating from that day.

CHAPTER 32

IN THE HOOSEGOW

After several more rides that continued to take us east, we decided to make our current ride the last of the day. Fortunately, the driver agreed to take us from the exit into town, a medium-sized community with a couple of traffic lights. It was now dark, it had just started to rain gently, and we were craving our next daily burger.

We started looking for a McDonald's or Burger King, but we had no luck in finding a burger joint. However, we spotted a hole-in-the-wall sandwich shop. Despite the sign in the front window, it might have been a stretch to call it a delicatessen.

We felt light raindrops as we entered the shop. Inside were several farmhand-type patrons and the sandwich-making guy, all getting excited about their college football team, expecting earth-shattering results this season. They said something about a "husker."

After a short discussion, we selected a sandwich we thought least likely to cause unrelenting diarrhea. We went outside to eat our bland, uninspiring half sandwich while sitting on the cement steps underneath the shop's awning. It was the only thing available to keep us dry. Now the rain was coming down harder, and dark clouds were rolling in. I heard the low rumble of distant thunder.

A dilemma was brewing. *Where do we find a dry place to sleep tonight?* It was unusual that we were considering sleep this early in the evening, but the limited amount of sleep we'd gotten the last night with the panel-van group was starting to take its toll.

We took turns taking drags off our last cigarette while contemplating our next move. All was not looking good.

I noticed that about two hundred yards down the road, there appeared to be a house. In the front yard was a faintly lit Police sign. I said, "Hey, let's check out that house with the Police sign. Maybe we can see if they have any ideas where we can go."

"Yeah, I guess so. We don't have much of a choice now."

Walking in the front door got us out of the rain. Water dripped from our clothes, forming puddles on the police department floor. A police officer sitting behind a desk was carefully evaluating us. I wasn't sure if he considered us bums, vagrants, or probable runaways, but regardless, he wasn't thrilled to see two boys or how our arrival was affecting his floor.

As Tommy and I approached the officer sitting behind the desk, I reasoned the seat could not have been big enough to accommodate both buttocks. Sometimes memories can be thoughts or feelings. My recollection of this meeting is purely visual.

I am sure his policeman's shirt size was XXXL. Despite the extralarge shirt size, the front buttons on his shirt stretched close to the breaking point; it was no mystery why the one missing button hadn't survived. A small dark brown growth protruded from his cheek's skin. It stood out so much that I struggled not to stare at it but instead focus on his entire face.

By that point in our trip, we'd accepted that when it came to speaking with law enforcement, my doing the talking was best if we wanted to avoid capital punishment. I told him our story, and he quietly listened before asking us his questions. Most of them were the same ones we consistently heard from everyone who stopped to give us a ride. Along with the questions and answers came an ID request. This occasion was about the twentieth time, and certainly not the last of the summer, when law enforcement needed to see our identification. I don't remember what I showed them; it could have been my library card[61] or perhaps my high school ID, neither of which had my address. Regardless, whatever I presented was never questioned.

I grew comfortable with Officer Chunky, as he seemed genuinely concerned about our predicament with the weather and our lack of funds.

---

[61] Most likely, this card had never been used in an actual library.

After consideration, he said, "If you want, I may be able to let you sleep here in the jail tonight."

Jail? Before then, I'd never thought of myself in the big house, but if it was a dry place to sleep, why not?

I glanced at Tommy with a look that said, *What do you think?* He responded with a nod of approval. I couldn't hide how grateful we were and how much we wished to take him up on his offer.

The officer had Tommy and me place our gear in a closet, less a couple of personal items, such as toothbrushes and our sleeping bags. I hoped our wet gear would dry out during the night. He then walked us over to the town's only jail cell.

Have you ever arrived at a hotel and, upon opening the door and viewing your new temporary home, thought to yourself, *Wow, this is nice.* I had the same reaction upon surveying our new lockup.

There were two beds, each with a small mattress on a platform, free of any metal parts or wires that an inmate could use to poke an eye out or commit suicide.

The cell was genuinely nice. How do I know it was an exceptional jail cell? Since that is a story from a different hitchhiking trip, I'll reserve it for another time.

Other noticeable accouterments included sheets, blankets, and a pillow with a clean pillowcase. Since our sleeping bags didn't come with pillows, resting my head on one would be a treat.

We must have hit the executive suite of brigs!

The rest of the jail cell included the standard three cinder-block walls; one wall of reinforced, thick steel bars; and a brushed-steel toilet, minus the seat (so you couldn't hit yourself over the head and kill yourself), with the matching brushed-steel sink, and of course, the cell was completely windowless.

The officer was like an armed bellhop, complete with the uniform, ensuring we were comfortable. He left us alone, returning to the chair and desk only fifteen feet away. We had a clear view of one another.

As we were preparing to lie down on our bunks, the police officer got up from his desk, grabbed a couple of items, and walked to the jail cell. He handed us each a jelly doughnut with white powdered sugar on top. Wow, the cop in this Nebraska town turned out to be one fine man.

The doughnut was good and brought the special feeling you get, like when eating your favorite dessert. It made an excellent dessert after the mediocre half sandwich we'd had as our daily meal. The box on his desk from which the doughnuts originated was sizable. I didn't picture him as the kind of guy to let food go to waste, which illuminated the reason for his respectable figure.

Besides giving us a dry place to sleep for the night, he must have decided there was no reason to close the jail cell door, as he left it open for the night. Sometimes it's what's not spoken that speaks the loudest; in this case, I think his actions came from compassion.

This small-time Nebraska jail kept some lights on all night. Among other reasons, I heard it said that inmates, mainly those convicted of indecent exposure, prostitution, jaywalking, and public urination, might like to read late. This proclivity is even more prevalent with female inmates, excluding the rapists. I have it on credible authority that assault-and-battery and other violent-crime felons, at least those who can read, are overwhelmingly voracious readers; however, they do it during the day in the penitentiary library.

In the morning, we woke by ourselves. The police were nice enough to let us sleep in. It was now time to get up and greet the new day with a smile.[62] A younger officer had replaced our doughnut-sharing friend during the night. He kept a curious eye on us as we gathered our few personal items and rolled up our sleeping bags, and we took advantage of using the bathroom before collecting our knapsacks from the closet.

I said good morning to the younger new replacement police officer; he acknowledged me by giving me a slight nod, indicating there would be no further conversation.

Evidently, breakfast wouldn't be part of the local complimentary stockade package.

As we left, I respectfully said, "Officer, we want to thank you for letting us stay here last night." Again, he just nodded.

Ah, a man of few words and even less personality. Unable to hold a candle to Officer Chunky.

---

[62] Later in my life, when waking my young children in the morning, I would greet them with "Time to wake up and greet the new day with a smile."

We walked out of the police station into a sunny day with a clear blue sky—a nice change compared to the night before.

We started our mile-long hike out to I-80 to begin a new day.

* * *

I-80 rolled past the outskirts of Lincoln, the capital of Nebraska, as we finally approached the eastern section of the state. Shortly after Lincoln, we went past Omaha, the preeminent city in the state. Nebraska was a vast state that seemed to go on forever. But like all good things, it eventually came to an end.

CHAPTER 33

IOWA OBSERVATIONS

A stone's throw past Omaha, a colorful sign welcomed travelers to the state of Iowa: "Welcome to Iowa: The Hawkeye State." I thought the sign's primary purpose was to welcome tourists, embrace them, and give them that special teddy-bear feeling. The sign's objective was commendable, but its success was questionable.

It's a grossly exaggerated rumor that people never go to Iowa. Let me cite some examples of people who go there.

Truckers travel through daily.

Candidates go there to campaign relentlessly every four years like clockwork. Iowans hear contenders continuously speak half-truths and make occasionally kept promises, all while bombarded with constant radio and TV campaign advertisements. Candidates endlessly shake hands and kiss babies as they make their rounds throughout the state.[63]

The candidates' campaigning bolsters Iowa's nominal GDP[64] with media advertisements, the printing of posters to be lined up on the side of every road the state, hotel accommodations, rental cars, and dialers generating massive quantities of recorded phone calls throughout the state.

Not that there is anything wrong with the state of Iowa, but seriously, can you think of a single attraction or any rationale for why you might

---

[63] When COVID arrived, the kissing part was modified to only holding them for a photo op, but I'm sure things will return to past proven tactics in due time.

[64] After the 2020 primary vote-count debacle, it's worth noting the significant uptick of calculator sales, most likely to ensure more accurate caucus vote counts in the future.

personally want to go there? I dare you—no, I double-dare you—to come up with one good reason.

I am going to help you out. Below are some reasons why you might consider going there:

- It has always been your dream vacation spot.
- It's your dream honeymoon destination.
- You wish to see cornfields.
- It hosts major sporting events.

   o You can attend an NFL football game.
   o You can attend a major-league baseball game, possibly even a World Series game.
   o You can see an NHL hockey game.

- It's a location to have your destination wedding.
- You can go snow skiing or snowboarding on one of Iowa's three mounds.
- You can do some butterfly watching.
- You can go mountain climbing (if you can find a mountain).
- You can go surfing.
- It's a place to quickly and easily boost the crime rate.
- You can join a caucus.
- You can enjoy the overwhelming number of available luxury restaurants.
- You can buy a perfect slice of New York pizza or a Philly cheesesteak.
- You can go scuba diving.
- You can go skateboarding.
- You can go whale watching.
- You can join the army.
- You can get superior medical care for a hangnail.
- You can go deep-sea fishing.

The list goes on and on. For more ideas and questions, contact the Iowa State Tourism Board at—oops, they don't have an 800 number. In 1970, the internet was still decades away; now, I suggest googling the phone number. I believe someone conceivably answered calls Monday through Friday, except for holidays, major 4-H Club meets, and the birthdays of the three friendly staff members.[65]

Iowa seemed to be all farmland. For hours, we rode past farms growing all kinds of crops. I would have known if it was weed or corn, but other than those, I had no idea what was growing in the fields.

Repeatedly, we saw signs proudly reminding people that Iowa produced more corn than any other state. Even if I'd carried around an abacus or handheld calculator (in 1970, they were priced around $400), I could never have counted how many times we saw reminders of Iowa corn production. For some reason, I saw more John Deere baseball-style hats in Iowa than anywhere else.

A John Deere cap on a rough wood board, displaying the green-and-yellow color scheme and the leaping-deer symbol. John Deere's leaping-deer symbol and John Deere are trademarks of John Deere and Company (iStock).

John Deere is the brand name of Deere and Company, an American company that manufactures tractors and other heavy equipment used in farming and other agricultural, construction, and forestry machinery. I understand if you're from the coastal states or a more urban environment and likely have no idea what I am referring to. This successful company primarily sells mainly farming and other heavy equipment worldwide.

My theory is that in Iowa, or any farming area in the United States, all males and females, many of whom chew and spit tobacco, most likely

---

[65] I acknowledge that things may have changed since 1970, and I have no infallible knowledge of the actual workings at that time.

own and wear John Deere hats.[66] In my experience, women tend to be cleaner with their habits, using a spittoon most of the time, which may result in more effective oral hygiene; thus, they tend to maintain more teeth than men.[67]

I can only conclude that every young man in Iowa, on or around his sixteenth birthday, is given a new John Deere hat with a mandate to last for the rest of his life. This lifetime event is the rite of passage to manhood. Some might call it the Bible Belt bar mitzvah.

It also is an unwritten rule that never, under any circumstance, shall the cap be washed or cleaned. I arrived at this conclusion by observing that the older the man or woman was, the filthier the hat was and, therefore, the more distinguished and revered the farmer was.

* * *

Somewhere in Iowa, a man stopped to give us a ride. After a few minutes, he told us a story: "I once picked up a hitchhiker, and he seemed like an all right kind of guy, but after a few miles, he asked me, 'Aren't you afraid I might be a serial killer?' I told him, 'Not really. The odds of two serial killers being in the same car at the same time are extremely low.'"

Besides the engine humming and the tires grinding down the highway, the car went dead silent.

Was this a warning?

Tommy and I looked at each other, stunned, speechless, and alarmed.

The driver then glanced at us with a smile that could only be interpreted as humorous. Taking a couple of seconds, Tommy and I absorbed what we'd heard and gradually relaxed, realizing he had gotten us.

---

[66] Note that this is not a proven fact tested using samples and statistical analysis.

[67] To prove my theory, I think an appropriate statistical analysis would be to sample dentists' input.

CHAPTER 34

THE BLACK MERCEDES

On another hot late afternoon in eastern Iowa, we waited for a ride that hopefully would finally take us across the nearby border into Illinois.

As we had done for most of the trip, we waited on the highway entrance ramp—in this case, for I-80 East. Cars slowed down at every ramp to navigate the turn, making it easier for vehicles to take advantage of the ample room to stop on the shoulder safely.

* * *

Hitchhiking is like fishing. Patience is required for each. Occasionally, you'll get a tug on the line when you're fishing. This tug tends to cause an immediate uplift in spirits, your heart starts beating a little quicker, and you respond by quickly focusing on reeling in that fish. The same reaction occurs when a car slows down or pulls over to give you a ride.

* * *

Wow, a black Mercedes-Benz pulled over to give us a lift. That was a first. We've never had an expensive luxury car offer us a ride before.

Some minuscule events, for some reason, remain in the brain's memory seemingly forever. For me, one of those memories is of opening that particular car door and seeing the car's sizeable interior as we stacked our gear in the backseat, still leaving plenty of space for Tommy to stretch out if he wanted to. I got into the front passenger seat and absorbed the immaculate, newish car with all the extras. It even had a new-car smell.

That same car now would qualify for historic plates if still on the road today.

Having never been in a Mercedes before, I soaked in the upscale car's dashboard containing dials and gauges, which I was fairly sure related to features.

The driver introduced himself as Sal. Sal was likely in his late thirties, with olive skin, styled black hair, and at least two days of beard growth. He wore some big-ticket casual clothes that fit perfectly with his expensive car. His clear pronunciation and vocabulary indicated a higher level of education. He was possibly a professional at something, and although he never told us what, we later came up with our own possibilities.

After getting into the touring car, we began our usual introductions, followed by the question-and-answer process we had done all summer. Sal was driving to Boston, which made this ride different from all the others on the entire trip—for the first time that summer, someone was going farther than we were!

* * *

It had been about twenty-four hours since we ate the doughnuts the cop in the Nebraska jail gave us, and we were starving. When Sal suggested we stop and get something to eat, we immediately agreed that was an outstanding idea.

Is he thinking of Burger King or McDonald's?

As we approached the Windy City, Sal said, "I know a place in town where we can eat." We took one of the many Chicago exits off I-80, driving north into the city's South Side. He seemed to know exactly where he was going.

Perhaps you have been to Chicago, maybe even numerous times, but I am going to guess you have never come close to the South Side unless you live there. Nobody intentionally goes there unless he or she

- o   is sufficiently armed,
- o   is wearing a Kevlar vest,
- o   is accompanied by a platoon of cops, or
- o   has a take-it-or-leave-it personal feeling about living.

This area impacts residents of all ages, including children walking on the sidewalks to and from school.

Growing up in the New York City area, I often was in the city. I felt comfortable there—most of the time anyway. The less comfortable exploits are stories for another time.

Since it was dark, I noticed that functioning streetlights were few and far between. That area of South Chicago looked like a collection of highly rough neighborhoods. Scary. Probably not the type of community you would suggest your grandmother live in unless she fits into the category of a gangbanging gangsta, bully, thug, or mobster proficient at using a semiautomatic or fully automatic handgun or assault weapon, including ample ammunition. All of these will help her maneuver these neighborhoods.

For those who live in this section of Chicago, a good day is not being a casualty of stray bullets flying through the neighborhood.

I was alerted when seeing the metal bars protecting each first-floor apartment window and the graffiti (some extremely vulgar) spray-painted on the walls of buildings, broken phone booths, mailboxes, garbage containers, and more. A finishing touch was observing the many parked or abandoned cars missing tires and wheels, most elevated on cinder blocks. Some of the cars undoubtedly had more than just the tires missing.

Oh, what episodes can happen here at night?

How naive I am—those same things are just as likely to occur in broad daylight.

I was sure that questionable local commerce and government entitlements supported South Side people, keeping both the rats and the people alive. I imagined the communities' needs were met by keeping people employed in various street-corner fields. I could only surmise that those fields encompassed illegal drug sales; gambling; available cash loans with no clearly defined interest rates, including highly motivating payback services (something that had to do with kneecaps); and all types of sexual prostitution. I'll leave the types to your imagination.

The brick-and-mortar commercial buildings included windowless strip joints, bars displaying tilted neon martini glasses, 24-7 bail bond services, and check-cashing locations with bars and bulletproof glass. Each venue had a neon sign, including the pawnshop and the Chinese takeout joint.[68] They all gave the appearance of legitimate business establishments.

Who knows what evil lurks in the hearts of men? The
Shadow knows (what goes on in this district).[69]

It was becoming dark when we arrived at the restaurant. Abundant lighting lit the parking lot. Surrounding the lot was a ten-foot-high wire fence topped with strands of barbed wire leaning outward. Ouch! The gatekeeper was a boxcar of a man managing the opening and closing of the gate, potentially packing large-caliber heat.

Why would they even need a fence?

I assumed it reassured patrons that their expensive high-end automobiles would still be there after their meal.

I glanced at part of the sign painted on the outside wall: "Steak and Seafood." My view from the car as we pulled into the parking lot made me think the napkins in this place might be worth more than our clothes.

As I got out of the car, the distinct smell of sizzling steak hit me. *Hallelujah!* I anticipated that this would be much better than the fast food burgers we'd been living on for the past two months. My mouth's reaction

---

[68] I noticed that the many malnourished cats seemed to stay away from the Chinese place.

[69] The Shadow first appeared on radio in 1930 as the narrator of CBS's *Detective Story Hour.* By 1932, the character was the star of his own show, and he soon became the hero, rather than the narrator. The Shadow was inducted into the Radio Hall of Fame in 1989.

to what I was smelling, plus imagining what it would be like to eat steak, activated my salivary glands—peppered with a hunger for food.

All of a sudden, a killer thought crept into my mind. The thought was such a threat that I had to calm myself down.

With a concerned look on my face, I said, "Hey, Sal, we really can't afford this kind of place," as we approached the entrance door.

He gave me a slight smile. "Don't worry—I've got this."

I was simultaneously relieved now that we weren't about to get our heads severed financially and thrilled with the anticipation of steak.

Clearing up the financial consideration ended the threat of washing dishes (and ending our good ride with Sal) or, worse, getting in trouble with the police.

The nice, upscale restaurant seemed out of place compared to the depressed district we were in.

The maître d' sported a black mustache as wide as his combined nostrils, remarkably resembling that of Adolf Hitler. He looked us over for a second, likely letting us in only because Sal's look matched the typical clientele dining there. Fortunately, we had left all our gear in Sal's car; otherwise, I was sure, we wouldn't have made it in. Most patrons were dressed appropriately in business-casual attire, making Tommy and I appear out of place—similar to local homeless surviving in this very neighborhood.

We were seated at a table for four. Each table had a properly placed ashtray; cloth napkins supporting clean, polished silverware; and a bottle of Lea and Perrins Worcestershire sauce as the solitary condiment, all on an elegant linen tablecloth.

The restaurant's inside walls were tastefully constructed from expensive natural wood, which added a sense of extravagance, vastly different from the paneling that was popular, blending perfectly with the serene carpet.

The interior ambiance consisted of tranquil piano background music and soft lighting, including lit candles at each occupied table. Comfortable chairs were soothing on the rear end,[70] and the sound of numerous hushed conversations was equaled only by the restrooms, which were clean enough

---

[70] I feel compelled to note the chair comfort here not as one suffering from extreme hemorrhoid discomfort but, rather, as someone who spent that trip sitting in car seats often challenged by bumps in the road.

to eat off the floor, albeit at that point in our trip, when it came to food, our hygiene requirements were set at a low bar.

In all probability, it was the first time we had washed our hands since Utah.

Thankfully, since Tommy and I came from a modern suburban area, our charming manners and etiquette appropriately fit the establishment, la-di-da!

The waiter arrived, left three menus on the table with a smile, and turned around to go—I assumed to give us time to make our selections—without even the obligatory "What drinks can I get you?"

Sal stopped him and said, "Three steaks, three beers, and a side of mashed potatoes." The waiter didn't need to write that order down. He asked for our preference for salad dressing and picked up the unnecessary menus.

The obligatory rolls showed up seconds later, along with the ceremonious lighting of our table candle.

The anticipation of the upcoming meal was killing me. Thankfully, it wasn't long before our waiter showed up with a stand supporting a large tray containing our meals. He precisely matched each plate correctly, including the drinks, with outstanding skill that could only come from experience. How impressive.

Hallelujah! Wow, what a meal! Real food. The flavorful steak looked and smelled good. It tasted even better.

Dammit, why did I eat so much of that bread? I wanted room for the steak. No worries. We found the space for the steak, leaving our plates clean.

Sal ordered another round of beers.

The check came. Sal glanced at it and reached into his pocket, retrieving a large roll of cash. I had never seen so many bills carried that way before. Many people carried money in wallets or billfolds, but that was my first time seeing a roll. My curious eyes focused on it, and I gradually concluded, although I did not know for sure, there must have been more than $1,000 in his hand—some difference compared to the roughly five bucks in my pocket.

He peeled off a couple of hundred-dollar bills and dropped them onto the check, and we left.

What a great guy. At the time, we would have nominated him for sainthood. He fed the poor and hungry.

That Chicago steak was the single best meal I ate over the seventy-five-day excursion. I can still savor it today.

If I were to see Sal now, assuming he is still alive and not encased in cement within the foundation of a Boston building, I would tell him again how grateful I was for that meal in 1970.

ROAMING THOUGHTS

After the genuinely satisfying steak dinner, back in Sal's luxury automobile, we eased into seats of satisfying comfort as we returned onto I-80. It was now completely dark as we proceeded eastward through Illinois and then into Indiana.[71]

As we entered Indiana, my thoughts drifted to the disappointment I'd experienced at the shitty way the Indiana State Police treated me as we traveled through the state on our way westward.

I am sure many fine people live in Indiana—many of whom aren't despicable. For me, Indiana is the one state that will always carry a negative connotation.

I'm sure some will say, "Hey, Bob, it was just one person—the cop—more than half a century ago. Get over it already!"

* * *

Memory is an exceptional function of the human brain. It is an essential tool we all use to grow and learn from birth. Memory use takes place in many everyday activities, including even simple tasks we take for granted, such as speaking, understanding everything we hear, many types of calculations, and every type of muscle movement our bodies can perform. For example, speaking a basic sentence involves memory of words, assembling words in a recognizable order, and verbalizing in a manner listeners understand. These

---

[71] Toward the end of the summer, the days were becoming noticeably shorter. On August 30, 1970, the sunset occurred at 7:27.

include timed breathing to push air past our vocal cords and coordinated mouth and tongue muscles to produce sounds. Ironically, we perform all these functions, and many more, automatically. Some people aren't conscious that everything we do uses memory within our brain and untold other related operations.[72]

A rhetorical question I have heard people ask is "Why can I clearly remember something from eons ago but not what I had for breakfast this morning?"

* * *

The Chicago steak meal we ate, right down to the details, is a remarkably clear memory of mine that has lasted for more than fifty years. If I entered the restaurant today, I could pick out the exact table where we sat, assuming the restaurant hasn't since been burned down for the insurance money, gone under due to COVID lockdowns, or failed to survive in that section of town.

I experienced the sensation I refer to as "a state of mind." I felt a peaceful state of mind while sitting contently in the car as we left Chicago. The rare contentment of a full stomach contributed much to the sensation.

Sal stayed focused on the road and kept his speed at an appropriate steady clip over the speed limit but never enough to attract a cop's attention.

Besides the dinner break, Sal had been driving steadily for hours. We had no idea how long he had been going before he picked us up. He never mentioned where he came from.

* * *

It was a pleasure to leave Indiana and see the welcoming sign "Ohio: The Buckeye State."

I-80 runs east and west along Ohio's northern section. A few miles north of I-80, on our left, was Lake Erie, one of the Great Lakes. Unfortunately, the darkness of the night prevented us from seeing anything.

---

[72] In today's world, this possibly is all taught and understood in the third grade. My civilian, nonprofessional comments on the brain and memory are opinions based on my personal observations.

The green reflective signs above the highway continuously reminded motorists that Cleveland was ahead.

At a certain point in Ohio, I-80 and I-90 merged for roughly a hundred miles running along Lake Erie, and then, shortly before Cleveland, they again separated.

Should we stay with Sal, riding on I-90, or jump off here and hope for the best on I-80?

We had to consider that this ride would take us a substantial distance of more than four hundred miles past Cleveland, dropping us off in the Albany, New York, area. We would then have to hitchhike another two hundred miles south of Albany to get home.

"Hey, Tommy, I see a bunch of signs. We need to decide which way we want to go. Normally, we would stick with I-80 since it would be the most direct way to get us home. I-90 continues east but ends up farther away from home."

"If it's OK with Sal, let's stay with I-90. It will suck if we soon have to find a place to camp or hitch another ride in the dark."

Sal, listening to the conversation, enthusiastically chimed in. "You guys are more than welcome to continue riding with me."

It took less than two seconds to make the easy decision to stay with Sal. Something happened when the three of us agreed to travel together. We bonded to a degree; maybe we became comrades on a shared journey and even started a new friendship.

Tommy and I didn't verbalize it, but other factors entered into the equation. We couldn't ignore the benefit of traveling in the supercomfortable Mercedes-Benz. Sal had given us an incredibly long ride; pleasant company; and a fantastic, philanthropic steak dinner. Consequently, with all thoughts shoved into the meat grinder, we stuck with Sal, passing I-80 as it headed southeast; for the second time that summer, we traveled on I-90.

Around that time, the first real thought of returning home hit me. On what date did school resume? I guessed we had three or four days, so no sweat; we'd make it home in time for the first day of school. Our exciting trip would soon end. I had mixed emotions.

How could this exciting summer have gone by so fast? I wonder what has been happening at home. I missed my parents and brothers.

* * *

I-90 veered to the northeast and entered Cleveland,[73] running close to the Lake Erie waterfront. Maybe it was the dark of night or because I was dozing at the time, but I had no memory of that city. That was a shame. I once had lived in Cleveland, in 1954, and had no recollection of it then either.

At the time, the decision to stick with Sal made sense.

Little did we know.

---

[73] Cleveland later would become home to the Rock and Roll Hall of Fame in 1983.

CHAPTER 36

"SURE"

Cleveland's lights gradually transitioned from suburbs to pitch-dark farm country. Somewhere around there, I drifted into dreamland as the outside world was in complete darkness. It was my first shut-eye since the jail cell in Nebraska.

I woke up to hear Sal saying, "Hey, Bob, you've been out for almost an hour."

I glanced toward the backseat to check on Tommy, who also appeared to be emerging from a nap.

I thought Sal must have had the stamina of Superman; he was still driving for an unknown number of hours.

When we both were awake, Sal asked, "You guys want to try some opium?"

It took me a while to absorb his offer. I had heard of opium before but was innocently unaware of it. I believe Tommy was as naive as I was.

My thinking at that point was *He's a nice, successful man who just treated us to an expensive, quality meal; plus, he is giving us a long ride very close to our destination.* I, with remarkable innocence, comfortably replied, "Sure."

* * *

We were on the New York State Thruway, in a remote area of the state—in every way, it was the complete opposite of New York City, where 43 percent of the state's population lives.

Sal pulled the Mercedes into a small rest area with about a dozen parking slots and parked the car. There were no buildings. We were the only car in the lot.

Sal turned around to have clear eye contact with us and seriously said, "I need to make absolutely sure that we have a clear understanding. I need you to promise me that under no circumstance will you ask me for more."

We assured him we would not.

He nodded, but obviously, our assurances were not good enough. Again, he more firmly repeated that we must promise not to ask for more, this time instructing us to say the words verbally. As we promised word for word at his direction not to ask for more, he took the time to look into our eyes. This method of promise now seemed to reassure him.

I was a little puzzled by the seemingly extreme assurance. For the first time, I thought the whole scenario was getting weird. In retrospect, I realize it should have started sounding internal alarms. For some reason, at the time, I wasn't at all concerned.

Sal reached over in front of me and opened the glove compartment. He pressed a lever on the left side within the open compartment, which opened another space—a secret hiding place. Since I was sitting in the passenger seat, I had a clear view of what turned out to be a professionally designed hiding place, a compartment external to the glove box, which I highly doubted was a dealer option.

He extended his hand and arm farther into the compartment and pulled out a gallon-sized clear plastic bag from its berth, simultaneously shutting the secret compartment and glove box door with speed and dexterity. He removed several items from the bag with practiced efficiency, including a small mirror of about four square inches. In addition to the mirror, he had a piece of clear glass the same size as the mirror. The last items out of the bag were several slender sticks. They were a solid light gray, and the largest was no more than six inches long.

Sal broke off about three inches of one of the twigs, returning the others to the bag. He broke the stick he was holding into a few pieces and placed them on the mirror. He carefully placed the glass and gently pressed the glass on top of the mirror. The result was instant: the stick pieces turned into light gray crystals—like fine grains of salt.

He returned the transparent glass to the bag and pulled out a plastic straw cut to about four inches in length. He skillfully took the straw and created two thin lines on the mirror. Tommy and I watched him go through the process as he looked up at us and said, "Here you go."

We gave each other an innocent look that said, *What's he talking about?*

Sal immediately recognized that he was facing two first-ranked amateurs who could stretch this longer than he planned to spend in the parking lot. He then guided us through the process of sticking the straw partway up one nostril while holding the other nostril closed and then inhaling a line of the powder up into our nose, all while carefully keeping the mirror level. He definitely didn't want any type of accidental spill.

Following his instructions, Tommy and I completed the procedure as he instructed.

I watched as Sal quickly replaced everything in the clear bag and then put the bag back into his secret hiding chamber off the glove compartment siding.

I noticed that Sal didn't participate.

I wondered to myself, *What is the big deal with this opium?*

Seconds later, I became aware that I felt as if I were floating comfortably on a personal cloud, possibly similar to how astronauts must have felt when weightless in space. I was in my own world, and everything was good. Free from even the slightest anxiety or concern, I floated in peaceful contentment.

You could have stuck a gun to my face and advised me that my head was about to be blown off, and I probably would have just smiled. Actually, I might not have heard, as I have no recollection of seeing or hearing anything during that bliss. If you had pulled the trigger, I doubt I would have felt a thing in my oblivion.

All was right with the world.

In my serene hypnotic trance, I didn't know what was happening outside my body, nor did I care. I existed in my own personal bubble. There was no discomfort of any type, nor could there be.

Sal said to me in a voice louder than general conversation, "Hey, Bob, are you OK? You haven't said a word in almost an hour." His words took me out of a haze, like waking up after a deep sleep in the morning.

An hour? I felt I had been in that ultrarelaxed state for an undefinable time—it couldn't have been more than mere seconds, although I had no idea. *Confusing.*

"Yeah, I'm fine," I responded as I returned to reality, and our conversation normalized. I could tell Tommy was going through the same reality-facing process. In a way, the normalcy was comforting, maybe because it was familiar and felt right.

Slam! At that moment in time, a life-altering experience happened.

I had to have more of that opium. I had to have it!

The feeling was beyond a craving or desire; it felt like a powerful need. The only thing that stopped me from asking for more was the repeated assurance I had given to Sal that I would not make that ask. Slightly more than fifteen minutes later, I felt that powerful desire ease back to normal. I felt a strong sense of relief. I couldn't have continued for long with that desparate feeling of need.

I never forgot those fifteen minutes and the terrifying feeling of opium's powerful grip on me. The out-of-control, radical must-have feeling of opium scared the hell out of me! It scared me to the point that I vowed never to let myself be exposed to it again. I held to that conviction. I didn't realize exactly how vital that life lesson would be at the time, but I think it ended up in the top three.

Having gone through that experience, I gained an insight into addiction that has lasted my lifetime. Considering the impact of our minor snorting of opium (I can't imagine what injecting this drug does), I now understand dependence and how addiction's consummate power could drag a human into the ultimate death spiral.

Outside of this being an event on the trip, my reason for telling this episode is for you: if ever tempted, you will know to make the intelligent decision never to use an opioid drug unless under a doctor's advice. Even then, be cautious.

For the love of God, avoid any chance of falling into the deadly, bottomless pit of addiction.

CHAPTER 37

NEW YORK STATE THRUWAY AT NIGHT

Sal looked over at me and said, "Bob, I'm too tired to drive. I can't do it anymore. Do you mind taking over for a while?"

"Sure." I didn't consider mentioning that I was too young to drive or didn't possess a driver's license.

I hopped into the driver's seat, quickly reviewed the shifter doohickey and turn-signal lever, and made a completely unnecessary adjustment to the rearview mirror. I thought these moves made me look like I knew what I was doing.

Since it was after midnight, the highway was quiet. I effortlessly pulled out onto the thruway. Wow, what a thrill it was![74]

After getting up to the appropriate speed, I remained focused to avoid causing any attention, such as exceeding the speed limit, considering my lack of authorization to drive and the possible "luggage" in the car.

Both Tommy and Sal were now sound asleep.

I was thrilled to be driving this nice, fancy car at a good clip. I qualified as a kid in a candy store.

All night, I drove east on the New York State Thruway across the entire state, and I eventually started seeing signs for Albany. Traffic was noticeably picking up as the sun began to rise. Sal and Tommy were still sleeping; now I began to feel tired. After passing a sign that said, "Albany

---

[74] On a personal note, I found myself in love with the feeling of the thrill. It was the feeling of a thrill more so than what initiated it. I'm sure everyone experiences this same sensation, but the degree of enjoyment varies widely.

15 Miles," I decided to pull into a rest area. The change in movement stirred the others from their sleep. As I pulled into a parking space and put the car into Park, Sal asked, "Where are we?" When I told him how close to Albany we were, he seemed genuinely impressed and said he'd resume driving, which was OK with me.

The three of us discussed a plan to arrive at the best spot for Sal to drop us off, considering our route home. Albany has a significant intersection of I-90 going east and west and I-87 going north and south; both are part of the New York State Thruway system. We planned to take the thruway offshoot (I-87 South) since that would take us to New Jersey—home.

We parted ways with Sal in the Albany area. Sal would continue east to the Massachusetts Turnpike (I-90), the most direct route to his Boston destination.

Now was our last chance to express our gratitude and extend Sal our sincerest thanks. We appreciated just about every person who gave us a ride that summer, but possibly, what we had been through over the previous sixteen hours made these thanks special. Sal had helped us cover a significant stretch of our trip, giving us the single longest ride by far.

* * *

We now stood at a major intersection of two busy interstate highways. It was Labor Day weekend, so traffic was particularly heavy, with vacationers trying to squeeze in the last few days of summer and taking advantage of the long weekend. The heavier the traffic was, the better it was for us— more potential rides.

CHAPTER 38

ARRESTED

Tommy and I became good friends, getting along fabulously the entire summer. But for the first time, near the end of our trip, we had a disagreement. It was over the best place to hitchhike from. The choices were from the ramp, my recommendation, or directly from the highway shoulder, Tommy's opinion.

In all fairness, I'll take the blame for the disagreement. I was tired and getting cranky due to driving all night and having no sleep.

This discussion occurred as we stood on the highway's shoulder, not hitchhiking or even close to any traffic, with our backpacks sitting on the pavement as we debated our options.

Our discussion suddenly came to a halt. We were distracted by a New York State police car that pulled over on the shoulder and stopped a couple of feet short of hitting us. The overhead lights were flashing.

Oh shit, nothing good can come out of this.

The officer got out of the car and walked over to get in front of us. The big man was in his thirties, had a military-style short haircut, was husky, and was very tall. Next to his official badge was a name tag: Biff Kaminski.

He looked us over carefully through his reflective sunglasses without saying a word, until he pointed to our knapsacks on the ground and said, "You boys have any drugs in there?"

Without a split second of hesitation, Tommy replied, "Yeah, man, we have a whole fuckin' pound."

What a reaction! In less than one second, the officer, in one fell swoop, grabbed each of us by the back of our shirts and threw us facedown on the hood of his police car. One second, I was standing; the next, I was lying on my stomach, looking at the lower windshield from the outside.

What just happened?

I was stunned, almost paralyzed, by the sudden loss of control.

With one hand, he grabbed each of us by the back collar of our shirt, dragged us off the car hood, and pulled us over to the side of the car farthest from the traffic.

Cars were now pulling over on the nearby ramp to catch a view of live police action.

Officer Kaminski had us place our hands on the car's roof, keeping our arms apart, and spread our legs. Finally, we were standing on the ground again.

He frisked us, seemingly disappointed at not finding any drugs, knives, or guns. With our backs to the officer, he handcuffed us to each other. I assumed he only had one pair of cuffs.

I would think it only fair that we got our own set of cuffs.

As I was in the process of being handcuffed, I got a glimpse of the ramp behind us, the same one we had been discussing hitchhiking from. I observed that at least eight cars were now parked on the ramp; people got out of their vehicles to view a police arrest in action. Several were taking photographs, and a few had their movie cameras out, filming exciting moments from their summer vacation!

The thought that this might be on the evening news occurred to me. This wasn't how I'd hoped to become noticed.

On TV, usually during news broadcasts, I had seen police pulling criminals into or out of police cars or removing them from buildings. The accused criminals were swarmed by reporters sticking microphones and video devices toward them while screaming indecipherable questions, desperate to document every detail of the perp walk.

Now I understood why the accused would disguise their appearance as much as possible. I could relate to the feeling of being photographed in the hands of police while handcuffed. It wasn't flattering and was not what my parents had hoped and dreamed for their firstborn.

Officer Kaminski opened the cruiser's back door and ushered us into the car, ensuring that he placed his hand on the top of our heads.[75] Even though I knew nothing about police procedures, I assumed this head-safety

---

[75] Was this step to avoid our injuring ourselves or a quick check for head lice?

process helped the handcuffed arrestee, who had limited maneuverability, get into the car. I also guessed this process must have been part of a course at the police academy.[76]

Once in the car, I had another opportunity to check out all the fans watching the police drama and taking in the action. At least five more cars had stopped on the ramp, allowing families to get out to see all the police activity. I could almost hear the cameras clicking.

Of all the different vehicles we had been in that summer, it was the first one with a cage-like metal divider separating the front from the backseat. I imagined the barrier was for combative prisoners resisting arrest, drunk and disorderly prisoners, mother rapists, and murderers with veins in their teeth, providing safety for the officer.

From a personal perspective, the cage prevented Tommy and me, already restrained, from climbing into the front to attack the officer, knock him unconscious, and steal his gun, all while handcuffed.

"Leave nothing to chance" might be the New York State Police motto.

People were still taking pictures with their Kodak and Polaroid cameras, which were probably handy for their Labor Day weekend activities. Cell phones with built-in cameras wouldn't be available for another thirty years.

Tommy and I were having our own perp walk without all the fanfare. I wasn't too concerned since we hadn't done anything wrong and didn't possess drugs, as the cop must have thought, based on Tommy's sarcastic faux admission.

While we absorbed all the attention we were getting, Officer Kaminski loaded our knapsacks and sleeping bags into the trunk of his cruiser. While pulling out into traffic, he picked up his police radio microphone and advised somebody that he had done a ten-this and ten-that, all of which was meaningless until I picked up a few words not in code: *two juveniles* and *narcotics*.

Oh no, what does that mean?

I knew that nothing good could come from the cop's use of those words. Tommy and I acknowledged hearing the trooper's words by looking at each other. Tommy was unusually quiet.

Shit, Tommy, look what you got us into now!

---

[76] For more interesting reading about police academies, I recommend John D. Drake and Kevin Kozak's *New Blue* (a Jerry Krone novel).

It was about a ten-minute ride to the state police barracks. The barracks were located between the northbound and southbound highway lanes, allowing easy access to the interstate from either direction.

Kaminski parked the car in the barracks parking lot near the building.

Four men in suits and ties stood in the lot, waiting for us.

I figured it was time to get out and thought I could get one hand over enough to pull open the door handle, but it wouldn't work. I concluded that the police car's door handle was broken. Not so. It took a minute for us to realize we were locked in.

After letting us out, Officer Kaminski cynically explained that police car back doors could only be opened from the outside. I assumed that was to prevent us from jumping out of the car at sixty miles per hour after being taken into custody for standing on the shoulder of a highway—although under different circumstances, this was a move I had taken into serious consideration in Wyoming earlier that summer.

Being handcuffed to each other made getting out of the car challenging. Officer Kaminski assisted us with the car-extraction process; however, it seemed the thought of unhandcuffing us didn't enter his mind.

The men in suits were introduced to us as state narcotics detectives. The big cheese, in the most expensive suit, was Lieutenant Gagleer. Maybe the perfect haircut with not a single hair out of place made the lieutenant the senior man in charge.

CHAPTER 39

PRELIMINARY SEARCH

Lieutenant Gagleer, Officer Kaminski, and the three other narcotics detectives walked us into the building. Walking as a group would possibly prevent the two sixteen-year-old boys from making a daring escape, despite being handcuffed to each other.

We were guided into a reasonably sized, air-conditioned room that was empty except for a large, heavy steel desk from the World War II era. It looked as heavy as a German Panzer tank. Based on its size and weight, it likely is still in the same place today. As with a deep golf swing, permanent divots in the linoleum floor tiles were probable.

Kaminski returned to the police car to retrieve our personal effects from the trunk. It took a couple of trips to bring it all to the interrogation room.

During that time, the detectives huddled around the desk, talking in lowered voices, I assumed to plan how they intended to handle us. Straining to hear what they were saying, I picked up a comment about a secretary rumored to be pregnant. Gossip had it the father was the commander, since the two seemed to be unnecessarily spending more time behind closed doors lately.

When all our stuff was in the room, Kaminski left, muttering something about his bladder and how he couldn't take it anymore.

He returned to the interrogation room, relieved, to see us still standing there. Kaminski said to the detectives, "Hell, couldn't one of you at least get them a chair?" Lieutenant Gagleer nodded to one of the junior detectives, who went into another room and then returned with two metal folding chairs that matched the same era as the ancient desk.

Then came one of the challenges the New York State Police faced: aligning the chairs to be spaced correctly and getting us seated simultaneously in a coordinated manner so that handcuffs were not unreasonably restraining. The seemingly relatively simple procedure became an almost comedically lengthy procedure.

Finally seated ten minutes later, we sat facing the desk, with the four detectives and Kaminski standing on the other side of it.

The strategically organized process began.

First, Lieutenant Gagleer examined each item. After completing his examination, he handed the item to the next detective, who went through the same procedure. It continued on down the line, with Kaminski being the final (lowest-on-the-totem-pole) evaluator.

Lieutenant Gagleer placed a knapsack on the desk and pulled out a sock, carefully examined it, tested the texture, and then pulled it inside out to check if something was hidden inside.

My knapsack had numerous side pockets of different sizes and various storage compartments inside and out. To ensure all items were checked, they completed the required inspection of all the compartments.

It went through my mind that this would move along quickly since they would soon tire of the stench emanating from the fatigued clothing worn day after summer day. No clothing had been washed since Cheyenne, Wyoming. Consequently, police sniffing techniques were kept at a minimum.

Lieutenant Gagleer shouted, "Got something!" Suddenly, the whole organized procedure fell apart in the excitement of the moment as each of the inspectors dropped what he was examining onto the desk and surrounded Lieutenant Gagleer to get a closer look at what he'd found.

It was a semibrown plastic bottle with pills in it. I could see in his eyes: *We got them with drugs.* He immediately opened the bottle while the others stretched their necks to get a good view.

The lieutenant looked at the label on the bottle, which showed the pharmacy, my name, the drug, the doctor's name, and dosage directions. To further his analysis, he emptied a few capsules into his hand to closely examine. Perhaps years of experience in chasing illegal narcotics made him realize the pills were legit. The lieutenant's face turned into a frown as he concluded this was nothing, so he passed the next guy, and they eventually put the bottle into the inspected pile, along with my reeking dirty socks and underwear.

Ah, the rush of the find got hearts pumping with adrenaline-induced excitement, only to be followed by inconsolable disappointment.

But wait—another find! This one was in Tommy's knapsack: the famed pocketknife from the first night out. Again, the whole team dropped what they were doing to inspect the deadly weapon. The lieutenant opened the knife and, looking at the dull blade, said, "Don't think it's long enough."

Long enough for what?

After a bit of discussion, one of the detectives hurried into an adjoining room and returned with a ruler. After holding the ruler against the knife blade for about one second, the lieutenant said, "Too short," and passed it on to the next detective.

It was close to an hour before they completed the examination of every item in both our knapsacks.

I was surprised when they found several of my items even I didn't know I had.

We were still sitting in our chairs, handcuffed, uncomfortable but somewhat relaxed, enjoying the free entertainment.

The crime-fighting group decided it was break time, so they left the room, probably to vent over not having found anything, leaving Tommy and me sitting alone in the brown steel chairs.

"Hey, Tommy, I am sure we're done here now. At least they should let us go soon."

"My wrist is starting to hurt from the damn handcuff. So is my arm, having to hold it in this awkward position. How are you doin'?"

"Yeah, my wrist is hurting too," I said. "I really want to get outa dis place."

Tommy asked me, "Why do you think this is taking so long? What are they doing?"

I muttered to myself, "I just don't know."

CHAPTER 40

PHASE TWO

With nothing happening, I took the time to study the handcuffs. I wasn't thinking about making a getaway, but I wanted to check them out to see how hard it would be to free myself. I was also curious, having never seen real handcuffs up close before.

After my careful evaluation, I knew we weren't going anywhere.

What happens if one of us needs to use the bathroom? Tommy and I had been through a lot that summer, and I was sure that one more obstacle wouldn't be insurmountable. Fortunately, there was no need to find out.

The force returned to the room to begin the unexpected phase two. This step involved a search of our sleeping bags. Going through each pair of underwear must have been difficult, but this phase turned out to be more physically challenging for the fine detectives, who may have felt a little overdressed for this part.

I guessed they had anticipated wrapping this up a lot quicker than they were. I had detective skills too.

Tommy and I watched as they unzipped both sleeping bags, laying them open and flat on the floor. The two open sleeping bags took up more than half the room.

Each cop made his examination, identical to the phase-one knapsack check. This one was different, however, because it involved getting on their hands and knees, bending their heads over to get their ears close to the sleeping bag, patting it down while listening, and using their hands to feel for anything out of place. Five sets of eyes, ears, and hands went over every square inch. The force stood around when the sleeping bag search was complete, again clearly disappointed. I assumed these law enforcement officers were now hoping the pain in their knees would end soon.

They had come up with zip, nada, nothing. The disappointment was evident as they whispered among themselves, likely pondering the next move. Although I couldn't hear what they were saying, I detected some disagreement.

Tommy and I might have been uncomfortable in the cuffs, but we were at ease in knowing they didn't have a damn thing on us.

As their brief discussion ended, they gave us a quick look and then left the room.

"Now I think they'll let us go," I told Tommy.

CHAPTER 41

PHASE THREE

At my tender young age and with my raw innocence, my experiences with law enforcement were limited. There is, however, one technique I now know about. I feel that disclosing this may break a highly guarded, seldom-used police code. The extreme code most likely goes like this: when all else fails, resort to phase three. This supersecret step presumably is known only by select law enforcement personnel.

Being civilians, we were wholly unfamiliar with phase three—hell, before that day, we hadn't been aware of phases one and two!

The group returned to the room a few minutes later and silently stood staring at us for what seemed like a long thirty seconds.

Then Kaminski announced, "I am going to take you boys one by one into the room next door."

Tommy shouted, "That's going to be pretty fuckin' hard to do when we're handcuffed to each other!"

The detectives and Kaminski appeared stunned by Tommy's trademarked lightning response.

It was hard to argue with the distinctly obvious.

The narcotics detectives left the room, never to be seen again.

Kaminski came over, unhandcuffed us, looked at me, and said, "You come with me," directing me into the adjoining room. He ensured the door was firmly shut.

The room was slightly smaller than our search room. The one item in this room was a table like those in a school nurse's office or a budget-conscious doctor's office, minus any stirrups.

He looked directly at me. "Kid, stand with your back against the wall." We then were face-to-face, a couple of feet apart.

In a serious tone, he directed me to remove my T-shirt.

An alarm bell went off inside. *Oh no, what the fuck is going on?*

Hesitantly, I followed his directions. I wasn't afraid, but I was getting razor-close and started feeling that this was getting a bit weird. I could handle whatever happened, I thought.

Kaminski moved a step closer and inspected my scalp in case I was hiding some contraband in my hair.

Nothing there.

He looked inside and behind both ears.

Nothing there.

Next, he asked me to open my mouth as wide as possible so he could get a good look. Not seeing anything worth arresting me for, apparently to be completely thorough, he had me elevate my tongue so he could get a good look underneath it, in case illegal substances were hidden there.

Nothing there.

Next, he said, "Kid, lift your arms, pointing to the ceiling." He then inspected both hairy armpits.

Officer Kaminski did not react to the whiff he must have gotten.[77] I was reasonably sure significant additional perspiration had started. Those armpits had to be odoriferous.

He didn't find anything there.

Kaminski's face got serious, and then, with a stern, raised voice, he said, "Strip naked, kid."

I looked him straight in the face and said, "What? Are you kidding me?" The look on his face said he wasn't.

I thought quickly, considering what had led to this situation, including the highway apprehension and the thorough search of all our possessions. I concluded this was part of the total shakedown. I felt he wasn't enjoying this any more than I was.

I removed my sneakers and socks as directed, followed by my pants and underwear. I recalled something my mother had repeatedly told me as a boy: "Make sure you are always wearing clean underwear. God forbid, if

---

[77] I am sure that carrying deodorant in our knapsacks was low on the priority list.

you ever had to go to the hospital, you wouldn't want to be caught wearing dirty underwear."

I couldn't have cared less what he thought of my underwear at that point.

I stood there stark naked.

I faced Kaminski as he took a quick look at my genitals. I guessed he didn't see anything too exciting, because he instructed me to turn around with my back facing him. I didn't think of it at the time, but that was when I should have been most concerned.

He didn't find any drug paraphernalia hiding on my back.

His next command was "Bend over."

Whoa, cowboy!

I turned around to face Kaminski, saying, "Bend over?" For the second time, I said, "You've gotta be kidding me."

He answered, "Kid, I don't like doing this either. Let's just do it and get it over with."

I was getting annoyed but believed him and turned back around.

He asked me to return to the bent-over position. "Now grab a hand on each ass cheek, and pull 'em apart."

What—no dinner and drinks first?

I believe there are some things I have to leave to the reader's imagination. This is one of them.

Thank God there was nothing there. That could have been uncomfortable.

When that day had begun, I hadn't expected to face a complete cavity search and full rectal exam.

When Kaminski finished inspecting all my possible orifices, I felt sure the intimate part of the inspection was over. Wrong.

We still had the podiatric exploration to go.

Kaminski had me sit on the tile floor, instructing me to extend my legs forward. The building air conditioning made the tile floor cold on my innocent, tender keister.

Now what?

Kaminski inspected the bottoms of my feet, and the only time he touched me was to move my toes slightly apart to see if I was hiding anything—like a kilo of illegal narcotics between my toes. After viewing all my toes, he stood and said, "OK, kid, you can get dressed, go back to your seat in the other room, and wait there." He opened the door to let me out and called Tommy into the same room I exited.

I didn't say anything to Tommy but did give him a roll of my eyes.

Tommy went through the same exam with the same outcome.

Suddenly, a thought hit me: the phase-three process had distracted me from appreciating the relief of being free of the handcuffs.

THE WHEELS OF JUSTICE

I figured we were finally done, so we proceeded to repack our knapsacks and roll up our sleeping bags since all our belongings were lying scattered on the floor. How thoughtless of our hosts.

I started thinking about how close the police barracks were to the highway. *We can easily walk across the parking lot and start hitching a ride home.*

We hoisted our knapsacks onto our shoulders and started walking to the door. We weren't aware that Kaminski had returned to the room to see us making our exit.

"Where the fuck do you think you are going?" Kaminski said firmly.

We then learned we were not entirely free to go just yet. There was another step, something I never anticipated: phase four.

Kaminski announced, "You boys are now going to court." His forceful tone assured us this step was not optional.

Kaminski ushered us to the same patrol car he'd used to bring us into the police barracks. This time, we weren't handcuffed. How trusting of him.

Again, he guided us into the backseat, only this time, he couldn't have cared less if we hit our heads on the car's body above the door. Without formal police training, I decided the prisoner-head-protection move only applied to those handcuffed at the time, but I certainly was no authority on the subject.

Kaminski put the car in Drive, left the barracks parking lot, and turned onto the highway. After about a mile, he took the first exit. It was a residential area. After several turns, the environment grew sparsely populated and heavily wooded. Houses were spaced farther apart as we traveled into the rural area.

During the ride, my mind was working overtime, considering all the possibilities we could face. We likely had gotten into this mess with the police due to Tommy's remark to Kaminski indicating we possessed drugs. I strongly felt that my doing the talking would indisputably benefit us both. I leaned over toward Tommy, whispering in his ear, "OK with you if I do the talking on this one?"

He silently nodded in agreement.

I had never been in a courtroom before. My only background with the court was what I had seen on *Perry Mason*.[78] The respected judge wore a black robe on TV, making the courtroom his kingdom.

Two tables faced the judge's elevated bench. The tables were the pulpits from which each side could present their arguments. Typically, one table was for the prosecutor, the one trying to prove the guilt of the crime, and the other table was for the defense, the one defending the person charged or accused of committing a particular crime against humanity—for example, hitchhiking.

Behind the tables were benches where the public could sit and watch the court proceedings to view justice being served.

There always was an American flag, usually close to the judge, as well as a depiction of Lady Justice—a blindfolded lady holding a scale.

In addition, a cop attending the proceedings mainly assisted the public with finding a nearby restroom. Other responsibilities included confiscating high-power automatic weapons and pipe bombs, escorting prisoners in and out of the courtroom, and stopping anyone who lost control or failed to follow the court's rules. I was sure there were other responsibilities I simply wasn't aware of.

Lastly, there was the jury, a panel of a dozen citizens from all walks of life. The jury's job was to collectively decide whether the accused was guilty or not guilty. The jurors sat in their own box, getting front-row seats to all the court action.

---

[78] *Perry Mason* was a legal-drama television series originally broadcast in black and white from September 21, 1957, to May 22, 1966. The title character, portrayed by Raymond Burr, is a fictional Los Angeles criminal defense lawyer.

Tommy and I were going to walk into this room alone. Who could help us? What exactly were we walking into?

I decided to try to look relaxed and confident, meaning I would play it by ear.

I can handle this.

Looking back today at this moment reminds me of the expression "In my youth, I knew everything, yet the older I grow, the more I realize how little I know," or something to that effect.

The ride continued taking us into an area where the only sign of life was the dense forest. Kaminski pulled the patrol car into a driveway of small stones that ran up a slight incline alongside an older home. The base of the house was elevated about thirty feet above street level. He put the car in Park and got out of the vehicle.

Hey, this is a plain house, not a courthouse. Did Kaminski have some other devious tricks for us?

Kaminski, our chauffeur, walked around to open the rear door so we could get out. How considerate of him.

We walked up the steps onto the porch, and Kaminski knocked on the front door. A woman in a housedress, probably in her seventies, answered the door. Upon seeing Kaminski, Mrs. Judge gave him a welcoming smile. Assuredly, she had been expecting his arrival, and this was not the first time they had met.

She accompanied us into her very lived-in living room in the older home. The dated furniture matched perfectly with the age of the house and its owners.

Our senses perked up when we discovered the enticing fragrance of home cooking. The aroma reminded me of how hungry I was. Our last meal had been the steak in Chicago.

All four of us were standing in her living room, when the judge entered the room unannounced. Instead of a robe, he wore a loud, short-sleeved plaid shirt with short pants supported by suspenders. The judge glanced at us, nodded at Kaminski to follow him into the kitchen, and gave his wife a loving smile. I knew Kaminski and the judge were talking about us, but the only thing I overheard was *hitchhiking*.

Mrs. Judge displayed photos of her happy family throughout the living room. Some showed embracing couples, some of those with children, and many showed past holidays and special family events. All suggested a loving family home.

Mrs. Judge didn't want to interfere with any of the proceedings. Still, hell, it unarguably was her home, so Mrs. Judge suggested Tommy and I make ourselves comfortable in their two living room accent chairs. Behind us was a picture window that looked out onto the front yard, street, and endless woods. A coffee table with at least a few decades of use sat between us and the sofa.

Mrs. Judge turned and walked into the kitchen.

I could not stop thinking about what I'd overheard: *hitchhiking.*

Wait a second. We were not hitchhiking when Kaminski stopped us. Yeah, we were talking about where to hitch a ride, but we were not hitchhiking at the time! If that was what we were being charged with, I knew we were innocent.

The judge entered the living room, carrying a legal-sized manila folder, with Kaminski nearby. He looked at us as if he approved of where we were seated. The judge placed his manila folder on the coffee table and sat down. He was the lone occupant of his living room sofa.

Before anything could start, Mrs. Judge came from the kitchen, carrying a plate full of freshly baked chocolate chip cookies and looking directly at Tommy and me. "Would you boys like a cookie?"

Ah, that was the homey scent that hit us when we walked in the front door.

There was no possibility she was offering the cookies to anyone other than us. With no hesitation on our part, we immediately accepted her offer. The small napkins she gave us with our cookies added a nice maternal touch. The cookies were still warm, and possibly, we helped ourselves to more of the cookies than appropriate; the quantity was commensurate with our hunger. Looking back, I realize our rapid consumption of the cookies may have accurately indicated poverty and malnourishment, conceivably invoking sympathy.

I decided Mrs. Judge was a lovely, sweet lady, and the fact that she was there in the room put me at ease a little bit.

It's amazing how you can remember those small things from a snippet in time from so long ago.

Mrs. Judge politely offered Kaminski and the judge cookies, but both declined.

With the distribution of cookies completed, the formalities began, with the judge in charge. Hey, it was his courtroom and house—literally.

Kaminski and Mrs. Judge stood in the living room, serving as prosecutor and gallery, intently watching everything.

No one announced the names of plaintiffs or defendants, whichever, and what happened to the all-critical docket number?

The judge began with preliminary questions for both of us, confirming our names, addresses, dates of birth, arrest records, left- or right-handed inclinations, tattoos, birthmarks, smallpox vaccinations, and more until he had sufficient detail to move on.[79] That part was easy.

Throughout the proceedings, I couldn't stop thinking that we hadn't done anything wrong.

Next, the judge proceeded to read some gibberish about sections, subparts, and codes, blah, blah, blah. I didn't have a clue what he was talking about.

The judge then explained that we had a right to have an attorney represent us. He paused. I paused.

I didn't even know how much a lawyer would cost and briefly wondered if the five singles I had left in my wallet would cover it. I doubted it. Considering we weren't there on murder charges, I decided we would take our chances. Hey, we hadn't done anything wrong in the first place!

Without any formality, I told the judge, "I think we'll pass on the lawyer."

Where is Perry Mason when you truly need him?

So far, Tommy was quietly doing an outstanding job displaying steadfast attention to the proceedings.

Then things got more serious.

The judge looked me in the eye and said, "You are being charged with the offense of hitchhiking. Do you understand this?"

I acknowledged with a "Yes."

Since I had been doing the talking so far, he looked directly at me and asked, "Will you be speaking on behalf of both of you?"

Again, I said, "Yes."

---

[79] DNA wouldn't be a tool used to prosecute criminals for another sixteen years.

The judge remained steady and serious. While I couldn't prove it beyond a reasonable doubt, I thought his wife was secretly praying for us.

Kaminski probably thought this was akin to a paid coffee break.

The judge hesitated and then, looking at me, asked, "How do you plead?"

Without any hesitation, I sincerely replied, "Innocent."

Everything went dead silent. The silence grew awkward. I could suddenly hear the clicking of a grandfather clock in another room.

The judge looked over at Kaminski and stared at him. For the first time that day, Kaminski looked unsure of himself. Kaminski quickly gave me a look somewhere between puzzlement and shock. I thought he was getting angry.

In the continuing silence, both the judge and Kaminski reverted to staring at me.

Mrs. Judge looked at all of us. I was sure she was thinking, *Oh, this is getting interesting. It'll be a hit at tea this afternoon. Louise and Gertrude will love this story.*

I realized that something serious was wrong, but what?

The silence continued. Everyone in the room was getting uncomfortable with the long pause. The judge took his eyes off me, shifted on the sofa seat, leaned his head back, and ran spread fingers through his gray hair, letting out a barely perceptible sigh. I thought the judge was somewhat dumbfounded and unsure what to say.

I pushed my brain into overdrive, trying to figure out what was happening. Then it hit me: I had said, "Innocent." No one here had expected that. *Why not just say, "Guilty"? What could they possibly do to us for hitchhiking?* I made a split-second decision and broke the silence by saying, "Uh, no, what I really mean is, uh, you know, guilty."

That changed everything.

The judge's shoulders relaxed as he let out a long exhale and straightened his sitting position on the sofa. Kaminski looked back into the living room at both of us, relieved.

In a less-than-sure voice, the judge looked at me and said, "In that case, I am going to fine you boys, um, two dollars apiece, but it doesn't have to be that; it can be lower. That fine is only if you have enough money to get home." He waited for our response.

How did he know we were on our way home?

I knew we could cover the outrageously unfair fine and agreed to the two-dollar penalty.

Apparently, the judge did not have a gavel to conclude the court session.

Tommy and I reached into our pockets, came up with the four dollars, and handed the money over to the judge. He pulled out a preprinted paper pad, wrote something on a page, and handed it to me.

It said, "Receipt $4.00," including the county name and date.

I kept that receipt for thirty years or so, but it eventually vanished like an unpaired sock, along with my ticket stub showing that I'd paid $3.75 to see Chuck Berry, B. B. King, and the Who perform at the Fillmore East in New York City in 1969.

Tommy kept his word and let me do the talking. I admired him and gave him the deserved credit for his teamwork in handling the court appearance.

My first time with the court was far from what I expected. As for my other later court experiences, well, I guess those are stories for another time.

Finished with the court, we thanked Mrs. Judge for the outstanding cookies and walked out the front door. It was then I realized we were in the middle of nowhere. *How are we going to get back to the highway?* A road in the wilderness like this probably didn't see more than five cars a day.

Fortunately, Kaminski offered the two convicted outlaws a ride back to the highway. Most likely, his good mood was due to the two arrests and two convictions he'd just added to his personnel folder, conceivably supporting his next raise and maybe even a promotion.

Kaminski said, "How about I take you guys to a ramp on the thruway? That's a good place to catch a ride."

We accepted the offer from the same guy who had arrested us and put us through atrocities, such as searching all our belongings, not to mention the bonus of a full-body cavity search, all under the false charge of hitchhiking. He was now driving us to a good place to hitchhike another ride.

Irony!

CHAPTER 43

DESTINATION: HOME

After trooper Kaminski dropped us off at a thruway entrance ramp, only a few minutes passed before we got our first ride. As the miles piled up and I became more aware that we were heading directly south toward home, a sense of anticipation slowly arose within me. It generated some energy; I sat up and leaned forward, willing the car to cover the miles faster.

After a few relatively short rides, an engaging man, maybe about forty, picked us up, and the conversation followed the usual course: "Where have you been? How long have you been traveling?" and so on.

We told him we had been on the road for seventy-five days and had traveled more than seven thousand miles. Just then, Tommy interrupted the discussion. Pointing out the window, he said, "Hey, Bob, look at that sign! 'Entering New Jersey!'" This was followed by an exciting exchange of thoughts between Tommy and me about what time we'd make it home and what difficulties we might have with local, nonhighway hitchhiking.

The driver jumped into our conversation. He must have been impressed with our hitchhiking feat, because he made us a fantastic offer: "Since you're so close to your homes, I'd be happy to drive you right to your houses." It was a great way to end our trip. We generously responded with words of appreciation.

He did his good deed for the day.

After getting out of the car, I carried my luggage to the front door. While the home was familiar, at the same time, I had a foreign feeling; perhaps it came from guilt for having been away too long. I walked in, calling names, trying to assess who was home. All was quiet; I was alone. Ah, I realized my family was probably at some Labor Day function.

I felt comfortable at home. I knew where everything was and knew my family would return soon. It hit me then just how much I'd missed them.

* * *

I took what might have been a record-length shower as I put some muscle into the scrub. I then dried off with a clean, fresh-smelling towel with a flower-garden aroma—probably inserted somewhere in the washing or drying process—and put on clean clothes. It was a great feeling.

More than fifty years later, I now wonder how much I weighed on that day, but unlike today, that number was presumably of no interest or concern then.

A raid of the refrigerator gave me another good feeling of being home. It was something I hadn't done over the last two and a half months.

After refueling, I collapsed onto my bed, feeling reunited with home's comfort, including my familiar, friendly bed and pillow. Lying on my back, looking at the ceiling, I started to think about my summer. I decided I would wait until tomorrow to unpack the knapsack of dirty clothes and miscellaneous items. *As for my now worn sleeping bag, if not cleanable, despite how good a companion it has been, well, it is probably time for it to go.*[80]

Upon my arriving home, the impact of the summer trip to California and back was one of a fun summer trip with many interesting and memorable events, but all in all, it was not necessarily a big deal. I recognized that my trip was unique at the time, but to my amazement, over the next couple of years, I learned that none of my friends had made a trip of this distance. The oddity of the adventure was not something my peers would necessarily relate to. That most likely explains why I didn't tell others any of these stories for more than two decades. I wouldn't realize the magnitude of what happened on this trip or talk about it until I was in my thirties.

After an explosive and exciting summer, it was good to be home!

---

[80] As it turned out, after a good washing, it lasted years longer.

CHAPTER 44

REMINISCING

I'd been on this planet for sixteen years, and that summer had been my most exciting time ever. I didn't recognize the impact it would have on me at the time, but I felt that summer had been special. Upon arriving home, I felt overwhelmed by the number of experiences that had occurred each day. Many of the incidents affected my senses, particularly my sight. I'd viewed many new and unexpected things for the first time. My emotions had swayed between the thrill of enjoyment and happiness and extreme fear caused by the threat of near death and—I'm not afraid to admit it— cockroaches. Truly the Wyoming hunting desperados terrified me. The gangsters challenged my values in the panel van traveling east from Utah to western Nebraska.

People showed us generosity and overwhelming kindness, which greatly affected me, especially at this age. Their benevolence impressed me. I am grateful to each person who gave us a ride on this lengthy trip. I estimate that the trip covered over 7,000 miles.

* * *

I learned much on this trip from the countless people we met and the exploits we lived through. I'm confident that what happened on this journey impacted who I am today.

In some undefinable respects, I'm sure some episodes from this trip helped me succeed throughout my sales and business career. Meeting numerous people expanded the lens of how I see others and, maybe even more important, taught me to listen and genuinely hear. With each ride, we met new people. All had their own stories about the day's events, their jobs, personal challenges, what they did for entertainment, and a wide range of emotions, all expressed in many different and unique ways. For example, the near-death gest with the two guys who pulled guns on us on the Wyoming ride gave me an unexpected life-changing appreciation for living.

I gained an education on the responsible use of money, including spending it wisely and the value of frugality. Also, the trip exposed me to real-world experiences, presumably making me wiser, although those who know me now may find that questionable.

Leaving to go on the trip, I was reasonably confident I knew my way around the country and understood it. I was wrong. That summer trip woke me up to the vastness of the United States of America, and I became a sponge, absorbing all the remarkable things we saw and experienced. Those impressionable experiences are the lifetime memories that make up this journal. I wouldn't trade this trip for the world. I feel very fortunate.

* * *

I wonder if the overwhelming natural beauty I saw in America still exists today. Possibly, over time, expanding construction of new buildings, significant population growth, additional shopping centers, increased manufacturing, and the evolution of more cars and trucks on roadways have stolen some of that natural beauty that overwhelmed me in 1970. It makes me wonder if prosperity, growth, and expansion are worth losing the beautiful environment I witnessed. I guess it depends on what is most important to each of us.

* * *

As I mentioned throughout, there were many times on the adventure when I breathed in fresh, clean air and not only noticed it but also genuinely appreciated it. I wonder how much of that is left in the areas we were in.

My friend Tommy was a super companion throughout the adventure, often adding fun, laughs, and excitement. We shared an exuberant and exhilarating summer that I never forgot. I continuously admired the remarkably quick wit he'd share with everyone, noting how it often played a crucial role in some of our exploits. Our relationship evolved as we branched off onto different highways throughout the remaining high school years and beyond.

As you may recall, on day two of our adventure, the four of us separated into pairs. We correctly agreed that would make procuring rides easier. Our planned meeting in Ohio never happened. Tommy and I did not stop at our planned rendezvous exit. I have to give Kevin and Fast Eddie credit for following the plan and waiting for us. Since we never showed, they became disappointed, to put it mildly, and hitched rides back home. I feel sorry that they missed out on all our adventurous escapades.

* * *

Besides the stories about the summer trip, I feel compelled to mention how our national parks impressed me. I know the trip inspired my respect for our National Park Service, particularly for safeguarding our precious, treasured land. I couldn't get over the incredible sights of America's natural beauty that the park system highlighted. I developed a respect for the wisdom of our political leaders who established the National Park Service to preserve these cherished lands more than one hundred years ago.[81]

* * *

My three younger brothers, Tim, Pete, and John, each went on hitchhiking trips of their own crisscrossing the country. Perhaps wisely, they made their trips post-high school graduation. Hitchhiking was likely viewed differently when my substantially younger brother John took his journey by car and possibly covered the most ground.

* * *

I have ancestors who were born, lived their lives, died, and were buried in the same town or village. I consider myself fortunate that I had the chance

---

[81] I must note that I hesitated to use the words *political leaders* and *wisdom* since doing so is getting close to the definition of an oxymoron.

to see a good chunk of America and live through the adventures of the summer of 1970.

As I review all I've written here, I realize there are countless stories (many more than the ones in this journal) I can tell children, family, and friends. I hope they and any other readers will enjoy this book.

May God bless and keep you always.
May your wishes all come true.
May you always do for others
and let others do for you.
May you build a ladder to the stars
and climb on every rung.
May you stay forever young.
May you stay forever young.

—Bob Dylan

Printed in the United States
by Baker & Taylor Publisher Services